Under Fire- The Sanctity of the Traditional Biblical Home

Joshua Rhoades

Published by Joshua Paul Rhoades, 2024.

While every precaution has been taken in the preparation of this book, the publisher assumes no responsibility for errors or omissions, or for damages resulting from the use of the information contained herein.

UNDER FIRE- THE SANCTITY OF THE TRADITIONAL BIBLICAL HOME

First edition. August 22, 2024.

ISBN: 979-8227178411

Written by Joshua Rhoades.

Also by Joshua Rhoades

Courage Under Fire: David's Stand On The Battlefield
Jonah's Journey: Voices Of Redemption And Lessons In Obedience
The Furnace Of Faith: 12 Principles From The Heat Of Faith
Whispers of Hope: Inspiring Stories of Men's Prayers In Scripture
Frontier Legends: The Oregon Dream
Elijah: A Beacon Of Boldness
HOOK, LINE & SAVIOUR - Faith Reflections from Fishing
Driven By Faith: Motor Racing Inspired Christian Life
30 Day Devotional - Bold and Strong- Coffee Devotions for a
Courageous Christian Walk
Authentic Christianity: The Heart of Old Time Religion
Flee Fornication: The Plea For Purity
Renewed Hope- How to Find Encouragement in God
Sounding The Call - The Voice of Conviction
The Altar - Where Heaven Meets Earth
The Sacred Art of Silence - How Silence Speaks in Scripture
Under Fire- The Sanctity of the Traditional Biblical Home
Who Is on the Lord's Side? A Call to Righteousness

Introduction
Chapter 1 - Marriage as a Covenant
Chapter 2 – The Husband's Leadership
Chapter 3 – The Wife's Respect
Chapter 4 - Children as a Blessing
Chapter 5 - Parental Responsibility
Chapter 6 - Sanctity of Life
Chapter 7 - Sexual Purity
Chapter 8 - Respect for Elders
Chapter 9 - Work Ethic
Chapter 10 - Honesty and Integrity
Chapter 12 - Hospitality
Chapter 13 - Forgiveness
Chapter 14 - Faithfulness
Chapter 15 - Modesty
Chapter 16 - Love and Sacrifice
Chapter 17 - Discipline
Chapter 18 - Humility
Chaptert 19 - Prayer
Chapter 20 - Scripture Study
Chapter 21 - Contentment
Chapter 22 - Respect for Authority
Chapter 23 - Gratitude
Chapter 24 - Unity in Christ
Conclusion

Introduction

In today's world, the idea of a traditional biblical home is being challenged like never before. What used to be considered normal and essential—the family structure as taught in the Bible—is now under attack. "Under Fire: The Sanctity of the Traditional Biblical Home" is a book that explores why this is happening, why it matters, and what we can do to protect and preserve the values that have held families together for generations.

The traditional biblical home is more than just a way of living; it is a foundation that God Himself established. From the very beginning, in the story of Adam and Eve, the Bible shows us that family is important. God created the family unit with specific roles for each member: husbands, wives, and children. These roles were meant to bring order, love, and stability into our lives. But today, these roles are often misunderstood, ignored, or even criticized. This confusion has led to broken homes, strained relationships, and a lot of hurt in our society.

This book is written for anyone who is concerned about these changes and wants to understand how to defend the traditional biblical home. It is a call to return to the values and principles that God gave us for our families. "Under Fire" discusses important issues that families face today, such as changes in how marriage is viewed, the loss of respect for parental authority, and the undervaluing of the roles of mothers and fathers. These are not just small changes; they are major shifts that can affect the health and happiness of our families.

One of the main ideas of this book is that the traditional family structure is not outdated or irrelevant. On the contrary, it is more important now than ever. The biblical model for the family is designed to bring out the best in each member, helping them to grow, thrive, and support one another. When we follow God's plan for our homes, we create an environment where love, respect, and understanding can flourish. But when we move away from these principles, we open the door to chaos and confusion.

"Under Fire" also provides practical advice on how to strengthen your family according to biblical teachings. It encourages parents to take an active role in guiding their children, couples to work together as partners, and everyone to recognize the value of their unique role in the family. It reminds us that the struggles we face are not new; people have always faced challenges in their families. But by staying true to God's word, we can overcome these challenges and build strong, healthy homes.

In a world that often seems to be moving away from the truths of the Bible, "Under Fire: The Sanctity of the Traditional Biblical Home" is a reminder of the power and importance of God's design for the family. It is a call to protect and cherish the home as a place where faith, love, and values are nurtured and passed on to the next generation. This book is not just about defending the family; it is about celebrating the blessings that come from living in a home that honors God's plan.

Chapter 1 - Marriage as a Covenant

In the beginning, when God created man and woman, He established marriage as a sacred covenant. Genesis 2:24 states, "Therefore shall a man leave his father and his mother, and shall cleave unto his wife: and they shall be one flesh." This verse teaches us that marriage is a union where a man and woman come together to become one in a lifelong commitment. This covenant is not just a social contract but a divine institution ordained by God. Today, however, the sanctity of marriage is under attack as society seeks to redefine it to include non-traditional forms, straying from the Biblical definition. For Christians, it is crucial to understand and uphold the original design of marriage as intended by God.

Marriage as a covenant involves several key principles that are essential for a Christian's walk with the Lord. First and foremost, it is about commitment. When a man and woman marry, they vow to stay together through all circumstances, reflecting God's unwavering commitment to His people. This commitment requires love, patience, and sacrifice, mirroring Christ's love for the Church. Ephesians 5:25 instructs, "Husbands, love your wives, even as Christ also loved the church, and gave himself for it." This love is selfless and unconditional, setting a high standard for marital relationships.

The idea of leaving one's parents and cleaving to one's spouse signifies the importance of prioritizing the marital relationship. This does not mean abandoning family, but rather, recognizing that the marital bond takes precedence. It forms the foundation for a new family unit, and this priority helps to create a stable and loving environment for any children that may come. The unity described as "one flesh" symbolizes a deep, intimate connection where two lives are intertwined in mutual support, respect, and love. It emphasizes the need for unity in all aspects of life, including spiritual, emotional, and physical.

In today's world, where marriage is often viewed as a temporary arrangement or subject to change based on personal desires, the Biblical concept of marriage stands in stark contrast. The redefinition of marriage to include non-traditional forms challenges the core of this sacred institution. For Christians, it is essential to hold firm to the Biblical teachings and model their lives accordingly. Upholding the covenant of marriage means resisting societal pressures and remaining faithful to God's design. This includes advocating for marriage as defined in Scripture and living out its principles in everyday life.

Marriage also involves a mutual respect and submission. Ephesians 5:22-24 says, "Wives, submit yourselves unto your own husbands, as unto the Lord. For the husband is the head of the wife, even as Christ is the head of the church: and he is the saviour of the body. Therefore as the church is subject unto Christ, so let the wives be to their own husbands in every thing." This submission is not about dominance or inequality but about harmony and order within the family, reflecting the relationship between Christ and the Church. It calls for a loving leadership from the husband and a respectful cooperation from the wife.

The attack on traditional marriage includes the normalization of relationships that diverge from the Biblical model. This can lead to confusion and a departure from the values that have historically upheld family structures. For Christians, it is important to respond with both truth and love. While standing firm on Biblical convictions, it is equally important to show compassion and grace to those who may not share the same beliefs. This balance reflects Jesus' approach of grace and truth in His ministry.

In practical terms, Christians can uphold the covenant of marriage by nurturing their own marriages and supporting others in theirs. This includes regular communication, prayer together, and seeking God's guidance in all decisions. It also means being a witness to the world of what a God-centered marriage looks like. By living out the principles of love, commitment, and unity, Christians can demonstrate the beauty and strength of a marriage that honors God.

Moreover, the covenant of marriage is a reflection of God's covenant with His people. Just as God is faithful and unchanging, so too should the marriage covenant be steadfast. Malachi 2:16 says, "For the Lord, the God of Israel, saith that he hateth putting away: for one covereth violence with his garment, saith the Lord of hosts: therefore take heed to your spirit, that ye deal not treacherously." Divorce is seen as a violation of this covenant, highlighting the seriousness with which God views marriage.

In conclusion, the Biblical principle of marriage as a covenant is foundational to the Christian faith. Genesis 2:24 provides a clear blueprint for this sacred union, emphasizing commitment, unity, and mutual respect. Despite the societal pressures and redefinitions, Christians are called to uphold and model the Biblical standard of marriage. By doing so, they not only honor God but also provide a powerful testimony to the world of His design and purpose for marriage. This commitment to God's Word in the area of marriage is a crucial part of walking faithfully with the Lord.

Chapter 2 – The Husband's Leadership

The Bible teaches that the husband is the leader of the family. Ephesians 5:23 says, "For the husband is the head of the wife, even as Christ is the head of the church: and he is the saviour of the body." This means that just as Christ leads the church, the husband is to lead his wife and family. This leadership is not about power or control, but about love and responsibility. Christ showed His love for the church by giving His life for it, and husbands are called to show the same kind of selfless, sacrificial love for their wives. In today's world, the role of the husband as a leader is often undermined. Many people believe that there should be no difference in roles between husbands and wives. However, the Bible's teaching on this matter is clear and provides a model for a healthy and harmonious family life.

In a Christian home, the husband's leadership is a reflection of Christ's leadership of the church. This means that his leadership should be marked by love, service, and sacrifice. Ephesians 5:25 says, "Husbands, love your wives, even as Christ also loved the church, and gave himself for it." A husband who loves his wife in this way will seek her good above his own, putting her needs and well-being first. This kind of love creates a safe and nurturing environment where the wife can thrive and the family can grow together in unity and love.

The husband's leadership also involves providing for the family. 1 Timothy 5:8 says, "But if any provide not for his own, and specially for those of his own house, he hath denied the faith, and is worse than an infidel." This means that the husband has a responsibility to work and provide for the physical needs of his family. This provision is not just about money, but also about ensuring that the family has what it needs to live a healthy and fulfilling life. This includes providing a home, food, clothing, and other necessities, as well as creating a stable and supportive environment for the family.

Another important aspect of the husband's leadership is spiritual guidance. Ephesians 6:4 says, "And, ye fathers, provoke not your children to wrath: but bring them up in the nurture and admonition of the Lord." This means that the husband has a responsibility to lead his family in spiritual matters, teaching them about God's Word and leading by example. This includes praying with and for the family, reading the Bible together, and encouraging the family to grow in their faith. A husband who leads his family in this way helps to create a strong spiritual foundation that can withstand the challenges and difficulties of life.

The husband's leadership also involves being a source of strength and support for his wife. Colossians 3:19 says, "Husbands, love your wives, and be not bitter against them." This means that the husband should treat his wife with kindness and respect, supporting her in her roles and responsibilities. This support can take many forms, such as helping with household chores, being a good listener, and offering encouragement and praise. A husband who supports his wife in this way helps to create a loving and harmonious home where both partners can thrive.

In today's world, the role of the husband as a leader is often challenged. Many people believe that leadership should be shared equally between husbands and wives, and that there should be no difference in roles. However, the Bible's teaching on this matter provides a model for a healthy and harmonious family life. When the husband leads with love, service, and sacrifice, the family can grow together in unity and love. This kind of leadership creates a safe and nurturing environment where the wife can thrive and the family can grow together in their faith.

The husband's leadership is also a reflection of Christ's relationship with the church. Just as Christ leads the church with love and selflessness, the husband is called to lead his family in the same way. This means that his leadership should be marked by love, service, and sacrifice. Ephesians 5:25 says, "Husbands, love your wives, even as Christ also loved the church, and gave himself for it." A husband who loves his wife in this way will seek her good above his own, putting her needs and well-being first. This kind of love creates a safe and nurturing environment where the wife can thrive and the family can grow together in unity and love.

The role of the husband as a leader also includes being a protector. 1 Peter 3:7 says, "Likewise, ye husbands, dwell with them according to knowledge, giving honour unto the wife, as unto the weaker vessel, and as being heirs together of the grace of life; that your prayers be not hindered." This means that the husband should protect his wife, both physically and emotionally. He should be her defender and her advocate, ensuring that she is safe and well cared for. This protection also includes being a source of emotional support, offering a listening ear and a shoulder to cry on when needed.

In a world that often undermines the role of the husband as a leader, it is important for Christians to hold fast to the teachings of the Bible. Ephesians 5:23 says, "For the husband is the head of the wife, even as Christ is the head of the church: and he is the saviour of the body." This verse provides a clear and unchanging model for the husband's role in the family. By following this model, husbands can lead their families with love, service, and sacrifice, creating a strong and harmonious home that reflects God's design.

The husband's leadership also involves making wise decisions for the family. Proverbs 3:5-6 says, "Trust in the Lord with all thine heart; and lean not unto thine own understanding. In all thy ways acknowledge him, and he shall direct thy paths." This means that the husband should seek God's guidance in all decisions, relying on His wisdom rather than his own. By doing so, he can make decisions that are in the best interest of the family, ensuring their well-being and happiness.

The husband's leadership is not about dominance or control, but about love and service. Mark 10:45 says, "For even the Son of man came not to be ministered unto, but to minister, and to give his life a ransom for many." This means that the husband's leadership should be marked by humility and a willingness to serve. By putting the needs of his family above his own, the husband can create a loving and supportive environment where everyone can thrive.

In conclusion, the Bible teaches that the husband is the leader of the family, a role that is marked by love, service, and sacrifice. Ephesians 5:23 says, "For the husband is the head of the wife, even as Christ is the head of the church: and he is the saviour of the body." In a world that often undermines this role, it is important for Christians to hold fast to the teachings of the Bible and model their lives accordingly. By leading with love and service, husbands can create a strong and harmonious home that reflects God's design and provides a powerful testimony to the world. This kind of leadership not only honors God but also helps the family grow together in unity and faith.

Chapter 3 – The Wife's Respect

The Bible teaches that a wife should respect her husband, and this principle is found in Ephesians 5:33, which says, "Nevertheless let every one of you in particular so love his wife even as himself; and the wife see that she reverence her husband." This verse highlights the importance of mutual love and respect in a marriage. The husband is to love his wife as he loves himself, showing care, kindness, and understanding. In return, the wife is to respect her husband, acknowledging his role in the family and honoring him. This mutual exchange of love and respect creates a harmonious and balanced relationship, which is essential for a strong and healthy marriage.

In today's society, the Biblical instruction for wives to respect their husbands is often disregarded. Many people view respect as something that must be earned or as an outdated concept. However, respect is a fundamental aspect of any relationship, and it is especially important in marriage. Respecting one's husband does not mean that the wife is less valuable or that her opinions and feelings do not matter. Instead, it means recognizing the unique roles that each partner plays in the relationship and valuing the husband's leadership and contributions.

Respect in marriage is a reflection of the respect that Christ has for the Church and the respect that the Church has for Christ. Just as the Church honors Christ's authority and follows His teachings, a wife honors her husband's role and supports his leadership. This does not mean blind obedience or submission to wrongdoing, but rather a respectful partnership where both husband and wife work together for the good of the family. Colossians 3:18 says, "Wives, submit yourselves unto your own husbands, as it is fit in the Lord." This submission is about partnership and cooperation, not about inequality.

A wife's respect for her husband is expressed in many ways, including through her words and actions. Proverbs 31:26 says, "She openeth her mouth with wisdom; and in her tongue is the law of kindness." When a wife speaks kindly and wisely to her husband, she shows respect and fosters a loving atmosphere in the home. Disrespectful words and actions can harm the relationship and undermine the husband's role, leading to conflict and division. On the other hand, respect builds up and strengthens the marriage, creating a foundation of trust and love.

Respect also involves recognizing and appreciating the husband's efforts and contributions. Just as husbands are called to love their wives and provide for them, wives are called to acknowledge and value their husbands' hard work and dedication. This recognition encourages and motivates the husband, showing that his efforts are noticed and appreciated. It also reinforces the partnership aspect of marriage, where both partners support and uplift each other.

In addition to verbal respect, actions also play a crucial role. A wife can show respect by supporting her husband's decisions and standing by him in difficult times. This support does not mean agreeing with everything without question, but it does mean discussing decisions respectfully and working together as a team. When a wife respects her husband's decisions and supports him, it fosters unity and strengthens their bond.

Respecting one's husband is also about trust. Proverbs 31:11 says, "The heart of her husband doth safely trust in her, so that he shall have no need of spoil." Trust is the cornerstone of any relationship, and in marriage, it is vital. A wife who respects her husband trusts his judgment and relies on him. This trust creates a secure and stable environment for both partners and their children, promoting a sense of safety and belonging.

In a world where respect is often conditional or based on performance, the Biblical instruction for wives to respect their husbands stands as a timeless principle. It calls for unconditional respect, rooted in love and honor. This kind of respect reflects the love and reverence that believers have for Christ and sets a powerful example for others.

Respecting one's husband also involves encouraging his spiritual growth. A wife who respects her husband will pray for him, support his spiritual journey, and encourage him to lead the family in faith. 1 Peter 3:1-2 says, "Likewise, ye wives, be in subjection to your own husbands; that, if any obey not the word, they also may without the word be won by the conversation of the wives; While they behold your chaste conversation coupled with fear." A respectful wife can influence her husband's faith through her godly behavior and support.

The attack on the Biblical instruction for wives to respect their husbands often comes from a misunderstanding of what respect means. It is not about inferiority or loss of identity but about honoring God's design for marriage. When wives respect their husbands, they align themselves with God's plan and create a strong, loving, and stable home environment.

In practical terms, showing respect can be as simple as listening attentively when the husband speaks, valuing his opinions, and appreciating his efforts. It can also involve supporting his goals and dreams, standing by him in tough times, and being his biggest encourager. These actions, though small, build up and reinforce the husband's role, creating a partnership based on mutual respect and love.

Respect also means addressing conflicts with grace and humility. Ephesians 4:2-3 says, "With all lowliness and meekness, with longsuffering, forbearing one another in love; Endeavouring to keep the unity of the Spirit in the bond of peace." When disagreements arise, a respectful wife handles them with patience and a willingness to understand, seeking to maintain peace and unity in the relationship.

Another aspect of respect is recognizing the husband's need for admiration. Just as wives need to feel loved and cherished, husbands need to feel respected and admired. This admiration can be expressed through words of affirmation and acts of kindness, showing that the wife values and honors her husband. This mutual exchange of love and respect strengthens the marriage and fosters a deeper connection.

Respecting one's husband is also about setting a positive example for children. Children learn from their parents' behavior, and when they see their mother respecting their father, they learn to respect others as well. This respect extends beyond the family to all relationships, teaching children the importance of valuing and honoring others.

In a culture that often promotes self-centeredness and independence, the Biblical principle of a wife's respect for her husband offers a countercultural approach that emphasizes partnership, love, and mutual honor. It challenges the notion that respect must be earned and instead presents it as a fundamental aspect of a healthy and godly marriage.

For Christian wives, respecting their husbands is a way to honor God and His design for marriage. It is an act of obedience and faith, trusting that God's plan is perfect and leads to a fulfilling and joyful marriage. By respecting their husbands, wives reflect Christ's love and set a powerful example for others.

In conclusion, Ephesians 5:33 teaches that a wife should respect her husband, and this respect is a vital component of a strong and healthy marriage. Despite societal pressures and misunderstandings, this Biblical instruction remains relevant and essential. By showing respect through words, actions, support, trust, and encouragement, wives can honor their husbands and create a loving and harmonious home. This respect reflects the love and reverence that believers have for Christ and sets a powerful example for others. In a world that often undermines this principle, Christian wives are called to uphold it, trusting in God's perfect design for marriage. By doing so, they not only strengthen their own marriages but also provide a testimony of God's love and wisdom to the world.

Chapter 4 - Children as a Blessing

The Bible teaches that children are a blessing from God, and this principle is beautifully expressed in Psalm 127:3, which says, "Lo, children are an heritage of the Lord: and the fruit of the womb is his reward." This verse highlights the value and significance of children, viewing them as a precious gift from God. In a Christian's walk with the Lord, recognizing children as a blessing is essential for building strong families and nurturing the next generation in faith. However, in today's world, there is a growing devaluation of children and family life. This devaluation manifests in various ways, such as the increasing acceptance of abortion, the neglect of children's needs, and the diminishing importance of family in society. For Christians, it is crucial to uphold the Biblical view of children and family, understanding their importance and treating them with the love and respect they deserve.

Children are described in the Bible as a heritage, meaning they are a legacy and a continuation of God's blessings. They are not a burden or inconvenience but a reward from God, given to parents to love, nurture, and guide. In Proverbs 22:6, we are instructed to "Train up a child in the way he should go: and when he is old, he will not depart from it." This verse emphasizes the responsibility parents have to teach their children about God's ways, instilling in them the values and principles that will guide them throughout their lives. By doing so, parents ensure that their children grow up with a strong foundation of faith and moral integrity.

In a world that often prioritizes personal success and material wealth over family life, the Biblical principle of children as a blessing calls Christians to a different standard. It challenges us to view children not as obstacles to our goals but as integral to God's plan for our lives. When we embrace children as blessings, we recognize the joy and fulfillment they bring, as well as the opportunity to shape future generations for God's glory. This perspective shifts our focus from self-centered ambitions to the selfless act of parenting, where we invest time, love, and resources into raising godly children.

The devaluation of children is evident in the increasing acceptance of abortion. Many view unborn children as mere tissue or an inconvenience, rather than recognizing them as valuable lives created by God. Psalm 139:13-14 reminds us of the sanctity of life, saying, "For thou hast possessed my reins: thou hast covered me in my mother's womb. I will praise thee; for I am fearfully and wonderfully made: marvellous are thy works; and that my soul knoweth right well." These verses affirm that each child is fearfully and wonderfully made by God, deserving of life and protection. As Christians, it is our duty to defend the sanctity of life and speak out against practices that devalue and destroy it.

Neglecting children's needs is another way society devalues them. In some cases, parents are so consumed with their careers or personal pursuits that they fail to provide the love, attention, and guidance their children need. Ephesians 6:4 advises, "And, ye fathers, provoke not your children to wrath: but bring them up in the nurture and admonition of the Lord." This verse highlights the importance of nurturing and instructing children in a loving and supportive environment. Children need more than material provisions; they need emotional support, spiritual guidance, and the assurance of their parents' love. By investing in our children's well-being, we reflect God's love and care for His creation.

The diminishing importance of family in society is also a sign of the devaluation of children. In many cultures, the traditional family structure is being challenged and redefined, leading to a breakdown in family relationships and support systems. Malachi 4:6 speaks of the restoration of family relationships, saying, "And he shall turn the heart of the fathers to the children, and the heart of the children to their fathers, lest I come and smite the earth with a curse." Strong family bonds are essential for the healthy development of children and the stability of society. When families are fragmented, children suffer, and the fabric of society weakens. As Christians, we are called to uphold and strengthen family relationships, providing a stable and loving environment for our children.

Children are not only a blessing to their parents but also to the community and the church. They bring joy, energy, and a fresh perspective to the body of Christ. Jesus Himself valued children and welcomed them, saying in Matthew 19:14, "But Jesus said, Suffer little children, and forbid them not, to come unto me: for of such is the kingdom of heaven." This verse highlights Jesus' love for children and His desire for them to be a part of His kingdom. In our churches and communities, we should follow Jesus' example by welcoming and valuing children, providing them with opportunities to grow in their faith and use their gifts for God's glory.

Investing in children is an investment in the future. By raising godly children, we ensure that the next generation will carry on the legacy of faith and continue to spread the gospel. Deuteronomy 6:6-7 instructs us, "And these words, which I command thee this day, shall be in thine heart: And thou shalt teach them diligently unto thy children, and shalt talk of them when thou sittest in thine house, and when thou walkest by the way, and when thou liest down, and when thou risest up." Teaching our children about God's Word and His commandments is a vital part of parenting. It is through this diligent instruction that we pass on our faith and values to the next generation.

In a world that often devalues children, it is important for Christians to uphold the Biblical view of children as a blessing. This means advocating for their rights, protecting their lives, and providing them with the love and guidance they need to flourish. It also means prioritizing family life, recognizing that our relationships with our children are among the most important and impactful relationships we will ever have. By valuing and investing in our children, we honor God and fulfill His command to nurture and train them in His ways.

One practical way to value children is by spending quality time with them. In today's busy world, it is easy to become distracted by work, technology, and other commitments. However, children need our time and attention to feel loved and valued. Proverbs 22:6 reminds us of the importance of intentional parenting, saying, "Train up a child in the way he should go: and when he is old, he will not depart from it." By prioritizing time with our children, we can build strong relationships and provide the guidance they need to grow into responsible and faithful adults.

Another way to show that we value children is by providing them with a godly example to follow. Children learn by observing the behavior of those around them, and parents have a significant influence on their children's development. Titus 2:7-8 says, "In all things shewing thyself a pattern of good works: in doctrine shewing uncorruptness, gravity, sincerity, Sound speech, that cannot be condemned; that he that is of the contrary part may be ashamed, having no evil thing to say of you." By living out our faith authentically and consistently, we set a positive example for our children to follow.

Disciplining children in love is another important aspect of valuing them. Proverbs 13:24 says, "He that spareth his rod hateth his son: but he that loveth him chasteneth him betimes." Discipline, when done in love and not in anger, helps children understand boundaries and develop self-control. It is a necessary part of parenting that teaches children the difference between right and wrong and helps them grow into responsible adults. However, discipline should always be balanced with love and encouragement, ensuring that children feel secure and valued.

The church also plays a crucial role in valuing children and supporting families. By providing programs and activities that cater to children and families, the church can create a supportive community where children can grow in their faith. Hebrews 10:24-25 says, "And let us consider one another to provoke unto love and to good works: Not forsaking the assembling of ourselves together, as the manner of some is; but exhorting one another: and so much the more, as ye see the day approaching." By fostering a sense of community and belonging, the church can help families navigate the challenges of raising children in today's world.

In conclusion, the Bible teaches that children are a blessing from God, and this principle is crucial for Christians to uphold in their walk with the Lord. Psalm 127:3 reminds us, "Lo, children are an heritage of the Lord: and the fruit of the womb is his reward." Despite societal trends that devalue children and family life, Christians are called to view children as precious gifts from God and to invest in their well-being and spiritual growth. By valuing children, protecting their lives, providing for their needs, and nurturing them in the faith, we honor God and fulfill His command to train up the next generation. This commitment to children reflects God's love and care for His creation and sets a powerful example for the world. As we embrace children as blessings and prioritize family life, we create strong, godly families that can withstand the challenges of today's world and shine as a testament to God's goodness and grace.

Chapter 5 - Parental Responsibility

The Bible teaches that parents have a great responsibility in raising their children, as stated in Proverbs 22:6, "Train up a child in the way he should go: and when he is old, he will not depart from it." This verse emphasizes the importance of guiding children on the right path from a young age. In today's world, many external influences try to undermine parental authority and responsibility, making it challenging for parents to fulfill their God-given role. However, understanding and applying Biblical principles can help parents navigate these challenges and raise their children in a way that honors God.

Parents are called to be the primary educators and role models for their children. This means teaching them about God's Word, instilling moral values, and demonstrating a Christ-like character. Deuteronomy 6:6-7 says, "And these words, which I command thee this day, shall be in thine heart: And thou shalt teach them diligently unto thy children, and shalt talk of them when thou sittest in thine house, and when thou walkest by the way, and when thou liest down, and when thou risest up." This passage highlights the continuous nature of parental teaching and the importance of integrating faith into everyday life. By doing so, parents help their children develop a strong foundation of faith that will guide them throughout their lives.

One of the significant challenges parents face today is the influence of secular culture. Television, internet, social media, and peers often promote values that are contrary to Biblical teachings. These external influences can undermine parental authority and lead children astray. Romans 12:2 advises, "And be not conformed to this world: but be ye transformed by the renewing of your mind, that ye may prove what is that good, and acceptable, and perfect, will of God." Parents need to be vigilant and proactive in guarding their children's hearts and minds against harmful influences. This involves monitoring what they watch, the websites they visit, and the company they keep. By doing so, parents can protect their children from negative influences and help them stay focused on God's truth.

Parental responsibility also includes discipline. Proverbs 13:24 says, "He that spareth his rod hateth his son: but he that loveth him chasteneth him betimes." Discipline is essential for teaching children right from wrong and helping them develop self-control. However, discipline should always be administered with love and not in anger. Ephesians 6:4 instructs, "And, ye fathers, provoke not your children to wrath: but bring them up in the nurture and admonition of the Lord." This means that discipline should be fair, consistent, and aimed at guiding the child towards better behavior. It should also be accompanied by teaching and encouragement, helping the child understand the consequences of their actions and how to make better choices in the future.

Another critical aspect of parental responsibility is providing a loving and supportive environment. Colossians 3:21 says, "Fathers, provoke not your children to anger, lest they be discouraged." Children need to feel loved, valued, and secure to thrive. Parents can create this environment by showing affection, offering praise and encouragement, and being involved in their children's lives. Spending quality time together, listening to their concerns, and supporting their interests are all ways to build a strong, loving relationship with children. This connection helps children feel secure and confident, knowing that they are loved and supported no matter what challenges they face.

Parents are also responsible for their children's spiritual growth. This involves not only teaching them about God's Word but also modeling a Christ-like life. Children learn by watching their parents, so it is essential for parents to live out their faith authentically. James 1:22 says, "But be ye doers of the word, and not hearers only, deceiving your own selves." Parents should strive to practice what they preach, demonstrating love, kindness, forgiveness, and humility in their daily lives. This authentic faith provides a powerful example for children to follow and helps them develop their own relationship with God.

Prayer is another crucial element of parental responsibility. Philippians 4:6 encourages, "Be careful for nothing; but in every thing by prayer and supplication with thanksgiving let your requests be made known unto God." Parents should regularly pray for their children, asking God to guide, protect, and bless them. Prayer helps parents entrust their children's futures to God, acknowledging that He is ultimately in control. It also allows parents to seek God's wisdom and strength in their parenting journey, knowing that they cannot do it alone.

In addition to prayer, parents should also encourage their children to develop their own prayer life. Teaching children to pray and guiding them in how to talk to God helps them build a personal relationship with Him. This practice can be incorporated into daily routines, such as praying together in the morning, before meals, and at bedtime. By fostering a habit of prayer, parents help their children learn to rely on God and seek His guidance in all aspects of their lives.

The external influences that undermine parental authority often promote a sense of independence and self-reliance that is contrary to Biblical teachings. Society encourages children to follow their own desires and make their own rules, leading to a lack of respect for authority and a disregard for parental guidance. Proverbs 29:15 warns, "The rod and reproof give wisdom: but a child left to himself bringeth his mother to shame." Parents must counteract this message by teaching their children the importance of obedience and respect. Ephesians 6:1-3 says, "Children, obey your parents in the Lord: for this is right. Honour thy father and mother; which is the first commandment with promise; That it may be well with thee, and thou mayest live long on the earth." By instilling these values, parents help their children understand the importance of authority and the blessings that come from honoring it.

Parental responsibility also extends to educating children about the dangers of sin and the importance of repentance and forgiveness. Romans 3:23 reminds us, "For all have sinned, and come short of the glory of God." Parents should teach their children about the reality of sin and its consequences, as well as the hope and forgiveness offered through Jesus Christ. By helping children understand their need for a Savior and guiding them in how to seek forgiveness, parents play a crucial role in their children's spiritual development.

In today's world, where the family unit is often fragmented and parents are pulled in many directions, it can be challenging to fulfill these responsibilities. However, the Bible offers guidance and encouragement for parents who seek to raise their children in a God-honoring way. Psalm 127:3-4 says, "Lo, children are an heritage of the Lord: and the fruit of the womb is his reward. As arrows are in the hand of a mighty man; so are children of the youth." This passage reminds parents that their children are a precious gift from God and that their efforts to train and nurture them are valuable and significant.

Parents must also be aware of the importance of their own spiritual health. They need to nurture their relationship with God to effectively guide their children. Deuteronomy 6:5-7 emphasizes the importance of loving God with all one's heart, soul, and strength and impressing these commandments on their children. By maintaining a strong spiritual life, parents can better lead by example and provide their children with a solid foundation of faith.

Furthermore, parents should seek support and community within the church. Hebrews 10:24-25 encourages believers to "consider one another to provoke unto love and to good works: Not forsaking the assembling of ourselves together, as the manner of some is; but exhorting one another: and so much the more, as ye see the day approaching." Being part of a church community provides parents with encouragement, accountability, and resources to help them in their parenting journey. It also offers children additional role models and opportunities for spiritual growth.

In conclusion, the Bible teaches that parents have a great responsibility to train up their children in the way they should go. Proverbs 22:6 emphasizes the importance of guiding children from a young age, promising that this training will have a lasting impact. Despite the many external influences that seek to undermine parental authority and responsibility, parents can find strength and wisdom in God's Word. By teaching their children about God's Word, instilling moral values, demonstrating a Christ-like character, and providing a loving and supportive environment, parents can fulfill their God-given role and raise their children in a way that honors Him. This commitment to parental responsibility not only benefits the children but also strengthens the family unit and reflects God's love and care for His creation. In a world that often devalues parental authority, Christians are called to uphold and cherish the Biblical principles of parenting, trusting that their efforts will bear fruit in their children's lives and bring glory to God.

Chapter 6 - Sanctity of Life

The sanctity of life is a fundamental Biblical principle that underscores the value and sacredness of every human life. This principle is clearly articulated in Exodus 20:13, which states, "Thou shalt not kill." This commandment, part of the Ten Commandments given by God to Moses, establishes the divine prohibition against taking innocent life. It reflects God's view that life is precious and must be protected. In a Christian's walk with the Lord, understanding and upholding the sanctity of life is crucial. However, in today's world, this principle is under significant attack through the acceptance of practices such as abortion and euthanasia, which undermine the intrinsic value of human life. For Christians, it is essential to stand firm on the Biblical teaching that all life is sacred and to advocate for the protection and dignity of every person from conception to natural death.

The sanctity of life is rooted in the belief that human beings are created in the image of God. Genesis 1:27 states, "So God created man in his own image, in the image of God created he him; male and female created he them." This verse highlights the unique and intrinsic worth of every human being. Because we are made in God's image, each life holds immeasurable value and deserves respect and protection. This foundational belief influences how Christians view and treat others, recognizing that every person, regardless of their stage of life or condition, reflects the image of God.

One of the most significant challenges to the sanctity of life today is the widespread acceptance of abortion. Abortion is the deliberate termination of a pregnancy, resulting in the death of an unborn child. Many justify abortion on various grounds, such as personal choice, economic reasons, or concerns about the quality of life for the child or mother. However, the Bible consistently affirms the value of life from conception. Psalm 139:13-16 beautifully expresses God's intimate involvement in the creation of life: "For thou hast possessed my reins:

thou hast covered me in my mother's womb. I will praise thee; for I am fearfully and wonderfully made: marvellous are thy works; and that my soul knoweth right well. My substance was not hid from thee, when I was made in secret, and curiously wrought in the lowest parts of the earth. Thine eyes did see my substance, yet being unperfect; and in thy book all my members were written, which in continuance were fashioned, when as yet there was none of them." These verses reveal that God knows and values each person even before they are born, highlighting the sanctity of unborn life.

The acceptance of abortion represents a profound moral and spiritual crisis. By terminating an innocent life, society disregards the inherent value that God places on every human being. For Christians, it is essential to advocate for the protection of the unborn and to support measures that provide alternatives to abortion, such as adoption and comprehensive support for pregnant women. Proverbs 31:8-9 calls believers to speak up for those who cannot speak for themselves: "Open thy mouth for the dumb in the cause of all such as are appointed to destruction. Open thy mouth, judge righteously, and plead the cause of the poor and needy." This directive includes defending the rights of the unborn, who are among the most vulnerable members of society.

Another challenge to the sanctity of life is the growing acceptance of euthanasia, or assisted suicide. Euthanasia involves intentionally ending a person's life to relieve suffering, often for those with terminal illnesses or severe disabilities. While some argue that euthanasia is a compassionate response to suffering, it fundamentally contradicts the Biblical principle that life is sacred and only God has the authority to end it. Job 1:21 acknowledges God's sovereignty over life and death: "The Lord gave, and the Lord hath taken away; blessed be the name of the Lord." Taking life into human hands, whether through abortion or euthanasia, usurps God's authority and undermines the sanctity of life.

Christians are called to uphold the sanctity of life by providing compassionate care and support for those who are suffering. This includes advocating for high-quality palliative care, which focuses on relieving pain and providing emotional and spiritual support for those with serious illnesses. James 1:27 emphasizes the importance of caring for the vulnerable: "Pure religion and undefiled before God and the Father is this, To visit the fatherless and widows in their affliction, and to keep himself unspotted from the world." By showing compassion and care for those who are suffering, Christians can affirm the value of life and provide a powerful witness to God's love and mercy.

In addition to opposing abortion and euthanasia, upholding the sanctity of life involves promoting a culture of life that respects and values every person. This includes advocating for social and economic policies that support families, protect the vulnerable, and promote human flourishing. Isaiah 1:17 instructs believers to "Learn to do well; seek judgment, relieve the oppressed, judge the fatherless, plead for the widow." By working to create a society that values and protects all life, Christians can help to build a culture that reflects God's love and justice.

Educating others about the sanctity of life is also an important aspect of this calling. Many people, including fellow Christians, may not fully understand the Biblical basis for the sanctity of life or the implications of practices like abortion and euthanasia. 1 Peter 3:15 encourages believers to "sanctify the Lord God in your hearts: and be ready always to give an answer to every man that asketh you a reason of the hope that is in you with meekness and fear." By engaging in respectful and informed conversations, Christians can help others see the value of life and the importance of protecting it.

Prayer is another powerful tool in upholding the sanctity of life. Christians are called to pray for the protection of life, for those facing unplanned pregnancies, for those who are suffering, and for a change in societal attitudes towards life. Philippians 4:6-7 exhorts believers to "be careful for nothing; but in every thing by prayer and supplication with thanksgiving let your requests be made known unto God. And the peace of God, which passeth all understanding, shall keep your hearts and minds through Christ Jesus." Through prayer, Christians can seek God's guidance and strength in their efforts to uphold the sanctity of life.

Furthermore, Christians can support organizations and ministries that work to protect life and provide support for those in need. This includes crisis pregnancy centers, adoption agencies, hospices, and advocacy groups. By volunteering time, donating resources, and raising awareness, Christians can make a tangible difference in the lives of those affected by issues related to the sanctity of life.

The sanctity of life also has implications for how we treat others in our daily interactions. Recognizing that every person is made in the image of God should influence our behavior towards others, leading us to treat them with dignity, respect, and love. Matthew 7:12, known as the Golden Rule, instructs us to "therefore all things whatsoever ye would that men should do to you, do ye even so to them: for this is the law and the prophets." By living out this principle, Christians can affirm the value of life in their relationships and communities.

In conclusion, the sanctity of life is a fundamental Biblical principle that emphasizes the value and sacredness of every human life. Exodus 20:13, "Thou shalt not kill," underscores God's command to protect and honor life. Despite the challenges posed by the acceptance of abortion and euthanasia, Christians are called to stand firm on the Biblical teaching that all life is sacred. By advocating for the protection of the unborn, providing compassionate care for those who are suffering, promoting a culture of life, educating others, and engaging in prayer, Christians can uphold the sanctity of life and reflect God's love and justice. In a world that often devalues life, it is essential for believers to affirm the inherent worth of every person and work towards a society that respects and protects life from conception to natural death.

Through their actions and witness, Christians can make a significant impact and honor the God who created and values every human life.

Chapter 7 - Sexual Purity

The Bible teaches that sexual purity is a vital part of living a life that honors God. Hebrews 13:4 says, "Marriage is honourable in all, and the bed undefiled: but whoremongers and adulterers God will judge." This verse highlights the sanctity of marriage and the importance of keeping the marriage bed pure. It warns against sexual immorality and infidelity, reminding us that God will judge those who engage in such behaviors. In a Christian's walk with the Lord, maintaining sexual purity is essential. However, in today's world, there is a widespread promotion of sexual immorality and infidelity. Society often encourages behaviors that are contrary to Biblical teachings, making it challenging for Christians to stay true to God's standards. Yet, by understanding and applying Biblical principles, Christians can navigate these challenges and live lives that honor God. Sexual purity begins with understanding God's design for sex and marriage. In Genesis 2:24, we read, "Therefore shall a man leave his father and his mother, and shall cleave unto his wife: and they shall be one flesh." This verse shows that God's intention for sex is within the context of a committed, lifelong marriage between a man and a woman. This union reflects the deep, intimate relationship that God desires with His people. It is a gift meant to be enjoyed within the boundaries of marriage, where it serves to strengthen the bond between husband and wife and provides a stable foundation for raising children.

Unfortunately, today's society often promotes a very different view of sex. The media, entertainment, and even some educational systems encourage a casual attitude towards sex, presenting it as merely a physical act with no need for commitment or emotional connection. This perspective leads to a range of destructive behaviors, including premarital sex, adultery, pornography, and other forms of sexual immorality. These behaviors not only violate God's commands but also harm individuals and families. 1 Corinthians 6:18-20 warns, "Flee fornication. Every sin that a man doeth is without the body; but he that committeth fornication sinneth against his own body. What? know ye not that your body is the temple of the Holy Ghost which is in you, which ye have of God, and ye are not your own? For ye are bought with a price: therefore glorify God in your body, and in your spirit, which are God's."

Christians are called to flee from sexual immorality and to honor God with their bodies. This means making choices that reflect God's standards and avoiding situations that could lead to temptation. For example, it is wise to set boundaries in relationships to maintain purity and to avoid consuming media that glorifies sexual immorality. Philippians 4:8 advises, "Finally, brethren, whatsoever things are true, whatsoever things are honest, whatsoever things are just, whatsoever things are pure, whatsoever things are lovely, whatsoever things are of good report; if there be any virtue, and if there be any praise, think on these things." By focusing on what is pure and honorable, Christians can cultivate a mindset that helps them resist temptation.

Accountability is also an important aspect of maintaining sexual purity. Having trusted friends or mentors who can provide support and encouragement can make a significant difference. James 5:16 says, "Confess your faults one to another, and pray one for another, that ye may be healed. The effectual fervent prayer of a righteous man availeth much." Sharing struggles with others and praying for each other fosters a sense of community and accountability that can help individuals stay on the right path.

In addition to accountability, Christians must rely on the power of the Holy Spirit to overcome temptation. Galatians 5:16-17 encourages believers, "This I say then, Walk in the Spirit, and ye shall not fulfil the lust of the flesh. For the flesh lusteth against the Spirit, and the Spirit against the flesh: and these are contrary the one to the other: so that ye cannot do the things that ye would." By walking in the Spirit and seeking God's guidance through prayer and Scripture, Christians can find the strength to resist sexual temptation and live in a way that honors God.

Sexual purity also involves guarding one's heart and mind. Proverbs 4:23 instructs, "Keep thy heart with all diligence; for out of it are the issues of life." This means being mindful of what we allow into our hearts and minds through our thoughts, media consumption, and relationships. By filling our minds with God's Word and focusing on His truth, we can protect ourselves from the lies and temptations of the world.

The promotion of sexual immorality and infidelity in society can lead to significant harm, including broken relationships, emotional pain, and even physical consequences like sexually transmitted diseases. It can also have a profound impact on one's spiritual life, creating a barrier between individuals and God. Isaiah 59:2 warns, "But your iniquities have separated between you and your God, and your sins have hid his face from you, that he will not hear." Sin, including sexual immorality, separates us from God and hinders our relationship with Him. Therefore, it is crucial for Christians to repent of any sexual sin and seek God's forgiveness and healing.

Thankfully, God offers forgiveness and restoration to those who turn to Him in repentance. 1 John 1:9 assures us, "If we confess our sins, he is faithful and just to forgive us our sins, and to cleanse us from all unrighteousness." No matter what mistakes we have made, God is ready to forgive and cleanse us, restoring our relationship with Him. This forgiveness is a powerful reminder of God's grace and a motivation to pursue purity in our lives.

Parents also play a crucial role in teaching their children about sexual purity. Proverbs 22:6 advises, "Train up a child in the way he should go: and when he is old, he will not depart from it." By educating children about God's design for sex and the importance of purity, parents can equip them with the knowledge and values they need to navigate a world that often promotes contrary messages. Open, honest conversations about sex and relationships, grounded in Biblical truth, can help children develop a healthy understanding of God's intentions and the importance of waiting until marriage.

In addition to personal choices and family education, the church community has a responsibility to uphold and promote sexual purity. This involves teaching Biblical principles about sex and marriage, providing support and accountability for individuals, and creating an environment where purity is valued and encouraged. Hebrews 10:24-25 says, "And let us consider one another to provoke unto love and to good works: Not forsaking the assembling of ourselves together, as the manner of some is; but exhorting one another: and so much the more, as ye see the day approaching." By gathering together and encouraging one another, believers can strengthen their commitment to purity and support each other in living out God's standards.

Moreover, Christians are called to be a light in the world, reflecting God's love and truth to others. Matthew 5:16 says, "Let your light so shine before men, that they may see your good works, and glorify your Father which is in heaven." By living lives of purity and integrity, Christians can set an example for others and demonstrate the beauty of God's design for sex and marriage. This witness can inspire others to seek God's ways and experience the blessings that come from living according to His Word.

In conclusion, the Bible teaches that sexual purity is essential for living a life that honors God. Hebrews 13:4 emphasizes the sanctity of marriage and the importance of keeping the marriage bed pure, warning against sexual immorality and infidelity. Despite the widespread promotion of sexual immorality in today's society, Christians are called to uphold God's standards and live lives of purity. This involves understanding God's design for sex and marriage, setting boundaries to avoid temptation, seeking accountability, relying on the Holy Spirit, guarding one's heart and mind, and educating the next generation. By doing so, Christians can honor God with their bodies, maintain strong relationships, and provide a powerful witness to the world. Upholding sexual purity not only strengthens one's walk with the Lord but also contributes to a healthy and stable society that reflects God's love and truth. Through God's grace and the support of the Christian community, believers can navigate the challenges of maintaining sexual purity and live lives that bring glory to God.

Chapter 8 - Respect for Elders

Respect for elders is a vital Biblical principle that underscores the importance of honoring and valuing the wisdom and experience of older generations. Leviticus 19:32 says, "Thou shalt rise up before the hoary head, and honour the face of the old man, and fear thy God: I am the Lord." This verse teaches us to stand in the presence of the elderly and to show them respect, which is connected to our reverence for God. In a Christian's walk with the Lord, respecting elders is crucial, reflecting a heart that values and honors the wisdom that comes with age. However, today's world often promotes disrespect and neglect of the elderly, treating them as burdens rather than blessings. For Christians, it is essential to uphold the Biblical teaching of respect for elders and to integrate it into our daily lives, thereby setting a powerful example for others.

One of the fundamental reasons for respecting elders is the recognition of the wisdom and experience they possess. Job 12:12 states, "With the ancient is wisdom; and in length of days understanding." This verse highlights that wisdom often comes with age and experience. Elders have lived through various seasons of life and have accumulated knowledge and insights that can benefit younger generations. By respecting and listening to elders, Christians can gain valuable guidance and learn from their experiences, avoiding mistakes and making wiser decisions.

The Bible provides numerous examples of the importance of respecting elders. In 1 Kings 12, Rehoboam, the son of Solomon, sought counsel on how to govern the people of Israel. The elders advised him to be a servant leader and speak kindly to the people. However, Rehoboam rejected their advice and followed the counsel of his peers, leading to disastrous consequences. This story illustrates the value of heeding the wisdom of elders and the potential pitfalls of ignoring their counsel. It serves as a reminder to seek and honor the advice of those who have walked the path before us.

In addition to valuing their wisdom, respecting elders involves caring for their physical and emotional needs. 1 Timothy 5:1-2 says, "Rebuke not an elder, but intreat him as a father; and the younger men as brethren; The elder women as mothers; the younger as sisters, with all purity." This passage emphasizes treating older men and women with the same respect and care as we would our own parents. Caring for the elderly includes providing for their physical needs, offering companionship, and ensuring they feel valued and loved. Many elderly individuals face loneliness and neglect, which can lead to depression and a decline in health. By spending time with them, listening to their stories, and showing genuine interest in their well-being, Christians can demonstrate God's love and compassion.

Neglecting the elderly is a significant issue in today's society. Many older adults are placed in nursing homes or assisted living facilities and are rarely visited by family members. This neglect can lead to feelings of abandonment and worthlessness. James 1:27 reminds us of our responsibility to care for those in need: "Pure religion and undefiled before God and the Father is this, To visit the fatherless and widows in their affliction, and to keep himself unspotted from the world." Visiting and caring for the elderly, especially those who are widowed or without family, is an expression of true religion and reflects the heart of God.

The command to respect elders is also tied to our reverence for God. Leviticus 19:32 connects honoring the elderly with fearing God: "Thou shalt rise up before the hoary head, and honour the face of the old man, and fear thy God: I am the Lord." Showing respect to elders is a way of honoring God, who created all people and values every stage of life. Disrespecting or neglecting the elderly dishonors God and disregards His commandments. By respecting elders, Christians demonstrate their obedience to God and their commitment to living according to His principles.

In addition to personal interactions, the church community has a role in honoring and supporting elders. Churches can create programs and activities that involve older adults, ensuring they remain an integral part of the community. Titus 2:3-5 instructs older women to teach and guide younger women: "The aged women likewise, that they be in behaviour as becometh holiness, not false accusers, not given to much wine, teachers of good things; That they may teach the young women to be sober, to love their husbands, to love their children, To be discreet, chaste, keepers at home, good, obedient to their own husbands, that the word of God be not blasphemed." This passage highlights the importance of intergenerational relationships within the church, where older members mentor and support the younger ones. By fostering these relationships, the church can honor elders and benefit from their wisdom and experience.

Respecting elders also involves advocating for their rights and well-being. Many elderly individuals face issues such as inadequate healthcare, financial instability, and abuse. Proverbs 31:8-9 calls believers to speak up for those who cannot speak for themselves: "Open thy mouth for the dumb in the cause of all such as are appointed to destruction. Open thy mouth, judge righteously, and plead the cause of the poor and needy." Christians have a responsibility to advocate for policies and practices that protect and support the elderly, ensuring they are treated with dignity and respect.

Another aspect of respecting elders is preserving and honoring their legacy. Many older individuals have contributed significantly to their families, communities, and churches. Remembering and celebrating their contributions helps to preserve their legacy and shows appreciation for their hard work and dedication. Hebrews 13:7 says, "Remember them which have the rule over you, who have spoken unto you the word of God: whose faith follow, considering the end of their conversation." By acknowledging and honoring the legacy of elders, Christians can inspire future generations to follow in their footsteps and continue their work.

Respecting elders also means learning from their faith and spiritual journey. Many older Christians have a deep and mature faith, developed through years of walking with the Lord. Their testimonies and experiences can provide encouragement and inspiration to younger believers. Psalm 71:18 expresses the desire of an older believer to share God's works with the next generation: "Now also when I am old and greyheaded, O God, forsake me not; until I have shewed thy strength unto this generation, and thy power to every one that is to come." By listening to and learning from the faith stories of elders, Christians can gain a deeper understanding of God's faithfulness and grow in their own faith.

In today's fast-paced and youth-focused culture, it can be easy to overlook or undervalue the elderly. However, the Bible consistently teaches the importance of respecting and honoring those who are older. This respect is not just about politeness or social etiquette but is deeply rooted in our relationship with God and our understanding of His commandments. By valuing and respecting elders, Christians reflect God's love and wisdom, strengthen their communities, and uphold Biblical principles.

In conclusion, respecting elders is a crucial aspect of living a life that honors God. Leviticus 19:32 instructs us to "rise up before the hoary head, and honour the face of the old man, and fear thy God." Despite the societal trend towards disrespect and neglect of the elderly, Christians are called to uphold the Biblical teaching of respect for elders. This involves valuing their wisdom and experience, caring for their physical and emotional needs, advocating for their rights, preserving their legacy, and learning from their faith. By doing so, Christians demonstrate their obedience to God, strengthen their communities, and set a powerful example for others. In a world that often overlooks the elderly, it is essential for believers to honor and respect them, reflecting God's love and compassion in all their interactions. Through their actions and attitudes, Christians can make a significant difference in the lives of the elderly and honor the God who values every stage of life.

Chapter 9 - Work Ethic

The Bible teaches that a strong work ethic is essential for living a life that honors God. In 2 Thessalonians 3:10, it says, "For even when we were with you, this we commanded you, that if any would not work, neither should he eat." This verse emphasizes the importance of working diligently and taking responsibility for providing for oneself and one's family. It highlights the principle that everyone should contribute through their labor and that laziness is not acceptable. In today's world, there is a growing promotion of laziness and entitlement, which stands in stark contrast to the Biblical teaching on work ethic. As Christians, it is crucial to understand and apply the principles of a strong work ethic in our lives, setting an example for others and honoring God through our diligence and responsibility.

A strong work ethic begins with understanding that work is a God-given task. From the very beginning, God assigned work to humanity. In Genesis 2:15, we read, "And the Lord God took the man, and put him into the garden of Eden to dress it and to keep it." This verse shows that even in the perfect environment of Eden, work was part of God's design for man. Work is not a punishment but a means through which we can fulfill God's purposes and bring glory to Him. By working diligently, we reflect God's character, as He is a God of order, creativity, and purpose.

The Bible is filled with verses that emphasize the value of hard work and diligence. Proverbs 12:24 says, "The hand of the diligent shall bear rule: but the slothful shall be under tribute." This verse highlights the rewards of hard work and the consequences of laziness. Diligence leads to success and leadership, while laziness results in subservience and lack. Proverbs 14:23 also reinforces this principle: "In all labour there is profit: but the talk of the lips tendeth only to penury." This means that hard work brings profit and benefit, while mere talk and laziness lead to poverty and lack.

In contrast, today's culture often promotes laziness and entitlement. Many people expect to receive rewards and benefits without putting in the necessary effort. This attitude can be seen in various aspects of society, from the workplace to the educational system, and even within families. The idea that one is entitled to certain things without having to work for them is contrary to Biblical teaching. Colossians 3:23-24 instructs, "And whatsoever ye do, do it heartily, as to the Lord, and not unto men; Knowing that of the Lord ye shall receive the reward of the inheritance: for ye serve the Lord Christ." This passage reminds us that our work is ultimately for the Lord and that we should approach it with enthusiasm and dedication, knowing that our true reward comes from Him.

A strong work ethic is also about being responsible and reliable. Proverbs 10:4 says, "He becometh poor that dealeth with a slack hand: but the hand of the diligent maketh rich." This verse highlights the importance of being diligent and responsible in our work. Being reliable means showing up on time, completing tasks to the best of our ability, and being trustworthy in all that we do. When we are responsible and reliable, we reflect God's faithfulness and integrity.

Moreover, work is not just about earning a living but also about serving others and contributing to the common good. Ephesians 4:28 says, "Let him that stole steal no more: but rather let him labour, working with his hands the thing which is good, that he may have to give to him that needeth." This verse emphasizes that our work should benefit others and that we should be generous with the fruits of our labor. By working hard, we can provide for our families, help those in need, and support the work of the church and other charitable causes. This selfless attitude towards work reflects Christ's love and compassion for others.

Another important aspect of a strong work ethic is perseverance. Galatians 6:9 encourages us, "And let us not be weary in well doing: for in due season we shall reap, if we faint not." This verse reminds us that hard work and perseverance will ultimately lead to a harvest of blessings. There may be times when we feel discouraged or exhausted, but it is important to keep pressing on, trusting that God will reward our efforts in due time. Perseverance builds character and strengthens our faith, helping us to grow in our relationship with God.

In addition to personal diligence, it is important to instill a strong work ethic in the next generation. Proverbs 22:6 says, "Train up a child in the way he should go: and when he is old, he will not depart from it." Parents and educators have a responsibility to teach children the value of hard work, responsibility, and perseverance. By setting a good example and providing opportunities for children to develop a strong work ethic, we can help them grow into responsible and productive adults who honor God with their lives.

The church community also plays a vital role in promoting a strong work ethic. Hebrews 10:24-25 says, "And let us consider one another to provoke unto love and to good works: Not forsaking the assembling of ourselves together, as the manner of some is; but exhorting one another: and so much the more, as ye see the day approaching." By encouraging and supporting one another, Christians can help each other stay motivated and committed to working diligently. The church can provide opportunities for service and ministry, allowing members to use their skills and talents for the glory of God and the benefit of others.

Furthermore, Christians are called to be witnesses in the workplace. Our attitude towards work and our behavior on the job can be a powerful testimony to others. Titus 2:7-8 says, "In all things shewing thyself a pattern of good works: in doctrine shewing uncorruptness, gravity, sincerity, Sound speech, that cannot be condemned; that he that is of the contrary part may be ashamed, having no evil thing to say of you." By being diligent, honest, and respectful in our work, we reflect the character of Christ and can influence others for the kingdom of God.

In addition to being diligent and responsible, it is important to maintain a balanced approach to work. While hard work is essential, it should not come at the expense of our health, relationships, or spiritual well-being. Ecclesiastes 3:1 reminds us, "To every thing there is a season, and a time to every purpose under the heaven." This means that there is a time for work and a time for rest, and it is important to find a healthy balance between the two. By taking time to rest and recharge, we can avoid burnout and be more effective in our work.

Maintaining a strong work ethic also involves trusting in God's provision. Philippians 4:19 says, "But my God shall supply all your need according to his riches in glory by Christ Jesus." While it is important to work hard and be responsible, we must also remember that our ultimate security and provision come from God. By trusting in His faithfulness, we can approach our work with confidence and peace, knowing that He will provide for our needs.

In conclusion, the Bible teaches that a strong work ethic is essential for living a life that honors God. 2 Thessalonians 3:10 emphasizes the importance of working diligently and taking responsibility for providing for oneself and one's family. Despite the promotion of laziness and entitlement in today's culture, Christians are called to uphold the Biblical principles of hard work, responsibility, and perseverance. By understanding that work is a God-given task, being diligent and reliable, serving others, and maintaining a balanced approach to work, Christians can honor God and set a powerful example for others. Additionally, by teaching the next generation the value of hard work and supporting one another within the church community, Christians can foster a culture of diligence and responsibility. Through our work, we can reflect God's character, influence others for His kingdom, and experience the blessings that come from living according to His principles.

Chapter 10 - Honesty and Integrity

Honesty and integrity are crucial values in the life of a Christian, reflecting the character of God and His truth. Proverbs 12:22 says, "Lying lips are abomination to the Lord: but they that deal truly are his delight." This verse teaches that God detests dishonesty and delights in those who live truthfully. In a world where dishonesty and deceit are often accepted or even encouraged, Christians are called to uphold the highest standards of honesty and integrity in all aspects of their lives. This includes being truthful in our words, actions, and relationships, as well as maintaining integrity even when it is difficult or costly.

Honesty begins with recognizing that God is the source of all truth. Jesus declared in John 14:6, "I am the way, the truth, and the life: no man cometh unto the Father, but by me." As followers of Christ, we are called to live in accordance with His truth and to reflect His character in our daily lives. This means being honest in all our dealings and avoiding deceit in any form. Honesty is not just about telling the truth but also about living truthfully, with transparency and integrity.

The Bible emphasizes the importance of honesty and integrity in many passages. Proverbs 11:3 says, "The integrity of the upright shall guide them: but the perverseness of transgressors shall destroy them." This verse highlights that integrity provides guidance and stability, while dishonesty leads to destruction. Living with integrity means consistently doing what is right, even when no one is watching. It involves making choices that honor God and reflect His character, regardless of the circumstances.

In today's society, dishonesty and deceit are often seen as acceptable or even necessary for success. Whether in business, politics, or personal relationships, the temptation to lie or deceive can be strong. However, the Bible clearly teaches that such behavior is wrong and displeases God. Ephesians 4:25 says, "Wherefore putting away lying, speak every man truth with his neighbour: for we are members one of another." As

Christians, we are called to speak the truth and to build trust within our communities.

Honesty and integrity are also vital for maintaining healthy relationships. Trust is the foundation of any strong relationship, and dishonesty can quickly erode that trust. Colossians 3:9-10 instructs, "Lie not one to another, seeing that ye have put off the old man with his deeds; And have put on the new man, which is renewed in knowledge after the image of him that created him." By being honest with one another, we build trust and strengthen our relationships, reflecting the new life we have in Christ.

Living with honesty and integrity also means being truthful with ourselves. This involves acknowledging our mistakes, taking responsibility for our actions, and seeking forgiveness when necessary. Psalm 51:6 says, "Behold, thou desirest truth in the inward parts: and in the hidden part thou shalt make me to know wisdom." God desires that we be truthful in our hearts and that we live with integrity from the inside out. This means being honest about our struggles and shortcomings and allowing God to transform us through His grace.

Integrity also involves being faithful to our commitments and promises. Matthew 5:37 instructs, "But let your communication be, Yea, yea; Nay, nay: for whatsoever is more than these cometh of evil." As Christians, we should be known for keeping our word and being reliable. When we make commitments, we should follow through, demonstrating integrity in our actions. This builds trust and shows that we are people of our word.

In the workplace, honesty and integrity are essential for maintaining a good reputation and witnessing to others. Colossians 3:23-24 advises, "And whatsoever ye do, do it heartily, as to the Lord, and not unto men; Knowing that of the Lord ye shall receive the reward of the inheritance: for ye serve the Lord Christ." By working with integrity and giving our best effort, we honor God and provide a positive example to our coworkers. This can open doors for sharing our faith and demonstrating the difference that Christ makes in our lives.

In business dealings, honesty and integrity are crucial for building lasting relationships and earning the trust of clients and partners. Proverbs 16:11 says, "A just weight and balance are the Lord's: all the weights of the bag are his work." This verse emphasizes the importance of fairness and honesty in business. Cheating, lying, or engaging in unethical practices may bring short-term gains but ultimately lead to loss of reputation and trust. By conducting business with integrity, we reflect God's character and build a foundation for long-term success.

The acceptance of dishonesty and deceit in society can make it challenging to maintain integrity. However, Christians are called to stand firm in their commitment to truth, even when it is unpopular or difficult. Romans 12:2 encourages, "And be not conformed to this world: but be ye transformed by the renewing of your mind, that ye may prove what is that good, and acceptable, and perfect, will of God." By renewing our minds with God's Word and seeking His guidance, we can resist the pressures to conform to the world's standards and live according to God's truth.

Honesty and integrity also play a crucial role in our spiritual growth and relationship with God. Psalm 15:1-2 says, "Lord, who shall abide in thy tabernacle? who shall dwell in thy holy hill? He that walketh uprightly, and worketh righteousness, and speaketh the truth in his heart." Living with integrity draws us closer to God and allows us to experience His presence more fully. When we are honest and transparent with God, we open ourselves to His transforming power and receive His wisdom and guidance.

Teaching the next generation about the importance of honesty and integrity is also vital. Proverbs 22:6 advises, "Train up a child in the way he should go: and when he is old, he will not depart from it." Parents and educators have a responsibility to model and teach these values to children, helping them understand the importance of living truthfully.

By setting a good example and providing opportunities for children to practice honesty and integrity, we can help them develop a strong moral foundation that will guide them throughout their lives.

The church community plays a significant role in promoting honesty and integrity among its members. Hebrews 10:24-25 says, "And let us consider one another to provoke unto love and to good works: Not forsaking the assembling of ourselves together, as the manner of some is; but exhorting one another: and so much the more, as ye see the day approaching." By encouraging and supporting one another, Christians can help each other maintain a commitment to truth and integrity. The church can provide accountability, teaching, and encouragement to help members live out these values in their daily lives.

Prayer is a powerful tool in our pursuit of honesty and integrity. By seeking God's help and strength, we can overcome the temptations to lie or deceive. Psalm 139:23-24 says, "Search me, O God, and know my heart: try me, and know my thoughts: And see if there be any wicked way in me, and lead me in the way everlasting." By inviting God to examine our hearts and guide us, we can grow in integrity and align our lives more closely with His truth.

Forgiveness and reconciliation are also important aspects of living with honesty and integrity. When we fail and fall into dishonesty, it is essential to seek forgiveness from those we have wronged and from God. 1 John 1:9 assures us, "If we confess our sins, he is faithful and just to forgive us our sins, and to cleanse us from all unrighteousness." By confessing our sins and seeking forgiveness, we can restore relationships and continue our walk with the Lord.

Living with honesty and integrity not only honors God but also brings numerous benefits to our lives. Proverbs 28:6 says, "Better is the poor that walketh in his uprightness, than he that is perverse in his ways, though he be rich." Integrity brings peace of mind, as we have nothing to hide and no fear of being caught in a lie. It builds trust and respect in our relationships, leading to stronger and more meaningful connections with others. It also provides a solid foundation for success, as others are more likely to trust and support those who demonstrate integrity.

In conclusion, honesty and integrity are fundamental values for Christians, reflecting the character of God and His truth. Proverbs 12:22 teaches that lying lips are an abomination to the Lord, while those who deal truly are His delight. Despite the acceptance of dishonesty and deceit in today's society, Christians are called to uphold the highest standards of truth and integrity in all aspects of their lives. This includes being honest in our words and actions, maintaining integrity even when it is difficult, and reflecting God's character in our daily lives. By living with honesty and integrity, we honor God, build trust in our relationships, and set a powerful example for others. Through the support of the church community, the guidance of God's Word, and the power of prayer, Christians can maintain a commitment to truth and integrity, drawing closer to God and experiencing the blessings that come from living according to His principles.

11. **Financial Stewardship**

- *Proverbs 13:11*: "Wealth gotten by vanity shall be diminished: but he that gathereth by labour shall increase."

Financial stewardship is an important aspect of living a life that honors God. Proverbs 13:11 says, "Wealth gotten by vanity shall be diminished: but he that gathereth by labour shall increase." This verse teaches that wealth gained through dishonest or frivolous means will not last, but wealth earned through hard work and diligence will grow. In today's world, irresponsible financial practices and materialism are common, often leading people away from God's principles. As Christians, it is essential to understand and practice financial stewardship, managing our resources wisely and using them in ways that honor God and further His kingdom.

First and foremost, it is important to recognize that everything we have comes from God. Psalm 24:1 states, "The earth is the Lord's, and the fulness thereof; the world, and they that dwell therein." This means that all our resources, including our money, belong to God, and we are merely stewards of these resources. Understanding this helps us approach our finances with a sense of responsibility and accountability to God.

A key principle of financial stewardship is earning money honestly and through hard work. Proverbs 13:11 highlights the value of gathering wealth by labor, as opposed to gaining it through vanity or dishonest means. Colossians 3:23-24 says, "And whatsoever ye do, do it heartily, as to the Lord, and not unto men; Knowing that of the Lord ye shall receive the reward of the inheritance: for ye serve the Lord Christ." This verse reminds us to work diligently and with integrity, as our work is ultimately for the Lord. By earning money honestly and through hard work, we honor God and set a good example for others.

Another important aspect of financial stewardship is avoiding debt and living within our means. Proverbs 22:7 warns, "The rich ruleth over the poor, and the borrower is servant to the lender." Debt can be a heavy burden, leading to stress and financial instability. By living within our means and avoiding unnecessary debt, we can manage our finances more effectively and avoid the pitfalls of financial irresponsibility. This involves creating a budget, tracking our spending, and making wise financial decisions.

Saving and planning for the future are also crucial elements of financial stewardship. Proverbs 21:20 says, "There is treasure to be desired and oil in the dwelling of the wise; but a foolish man spendeth it up." Saving money allows us to prepare for future needs and emergencies, reducing the likelihood of financial crises. It also enables us to take advantage of opportunities and provide for our families. By saving and planning for the future, we demonstrate wisdom and prudence in managing our resources.

Generosity is another key principle of financial stewardship. Proverbs 11:24-25 states, "There is that scattereth, and yet increaseth; and there is that withholdeth more than is meet, but it tendeth to poverty. The liberal soul shall be made fat: and he that watereth shall be watered also himself." This verse teaches that generosity leads to blessing, while selfishness leads to lack. By giving generously to others, we reflect God's love and compassion, and we trust in His provision. 2 Corinthians 9:7 reminds us, "Every man according as he purposeth in his heart, so let him give; not grudgingly, or of necessity: for God loveth a cheerful giver." Our giving should be done willingly and joyfully, as an act of worship and gratitude to God.

Another aspect of financial stewardship is avoiding materialism and the love of money. 1 Timothy 6:10 warns, "For the love of money is the root of all evil: which while some coveted after, they have erred from the faith, and pierced themselves through with many sorrows." Materialism and the pursuit of wealth can lead us away from God and cause us to prioritize money over our relationship with Him. Jesus said in Matthew 6:24, "No man can serve two masters: for either he will hate the one, and love the other; or else he will hold to the one, and despise the other. Ye cannot serve God and mammon." We must guard our hearts against the love of money and ensure that our primary focus remains on serving God.

Contentment is an important principle related to financial stewardship. Philippians 4:11-12 says, "Not that I speak in respect of want: for I have learned, in whatsoever state I am, therewith to be content. I know both how to be abased, and I know how to abound: every where and in all things I am instructed both to be full and to be hungry, both to abound and to suffer need." Learning to be content with what we have helps us avoid the trap of materialism and the constant pursuit of more. Contentment allows us to focus on what truly matters, such as our relationship with God, our families, and our service to others.

Stewardship also involves being faithful with the resources we have, no matter how much or how little. In the parable of the talents in Matthew 25:14-30, Jesus teaches about the importance of using our resources wisely. The servant who was faithful with what he was given was rewarded, while the servant who buried his talent out of fear was punished. This parable reminds us that we are accountable to God for how we manage the resources He has entrusted to us. By being faithful stewards, we honor God and are positioned to receive His blessings.

Another important aspect of financial stewardship is supporting the work of the church and other ministries. Malachi 3:10 says, "Bring ye all the tithes into the storehouse, that there may be meat in mine house, and prove me now herewith, saith the Lord of hosts, if I will not open you the windows of heaven, and pour you out a blessing, that there shall not be room enough to receive it." Tithing and giving offerings to the church support the work of ministry and help meet the needs of the community. By giving to the church, we participate in God's work and contribute to the spread of the gospel.

Prayer is an essential component of financial stewardship. James 1:5 encourages, "If any of you lack wisdom, let him ask of God, that giveth to all men liberally, and upbraideth not; and it shall be given him." By seeking God's guidance in our financial decisions, we can make wise choices and avoid the pitfalls of irresponsible financial practices. Prayer helps us stay aligned with God's will and rely on His provision, rather than our own understanding.

Teaching the next generation about financial stewardship is also crucial. Proverbs 22:6 advises, "Train up a child in the way he should go: and when he is old, he will not depart from it." By teaching children and young people about managing money wisely, earning honestly, saving, giving, and avoiding debt, we can help them develop good financial habits that will benefit them throughout their lives. This education prepares them to be responsible stewards of the resources God entrusts to them.

The church community plays a vital role in promoting financial stewardship among its members. Hebrews 10:24-25 says, "And let us consider one another to provoke unto love and to good works: Not forsaking the assembling of ourselves together, as the manner of some is; but exhorting one another: and so much the more, as ye see the day approaching." By encouraging and supporting one another, Christians can help each other stay committed to God's principles of financial stewardship. The church can provide teaching, resources, and accountability to help members manage their finances in a way that honors God.

Financial stewardship is not just about managing money wisely but also about recognizing the broader impact of our financial decisions. Proverbs 13:22 says, "A good man leaveth an inheritance to his children's children: and the wealth of the sinner is laid up for the just." This verse highlights the importance of thinking long-term and considering how our financial practices affect future generations. By being good stewards, we can leave a positive legacy and provide for our families and communities.

In conclusion, financial stewardship is an essential aspect of living a life that honors God. Proverbs 13:11 teaches that wealth gained through vanity will diminish, but wealth earned through hard work will increase. Despite the prevalence of irresponsible financial practices and materialism in today's world, Christians are called to manage their resources wisely, earning honestly, avoiding debt, saving, giving generously, and maintaining contentment. By recognizing that all we have comes from God and seeking His guidance in our financial decisions, we can honor Him and set a powerful example for others. Through the support of the church community, teaching the next generation, and relying on prayer, Christians can practice financial stewardship in a way that reflects God's principles and furthers His kingdom. This commitment to financial stewardship not only benefits us personally but also enables us to support the work of the church, help those in need, and leave a positive legacy for future generations.

Chapter 12 - Hospitality

Hospitality is an important principle in the Bible, highlighting the need to welcome and care for others, especially strangers. Hebrews 13:2 says, "Be not forgetful to entertain strangers: for thereby some have entertained angels unawares." This verse teaches that showing hospitality can have unexpected blessings, as we might be serving God's messengers without even knowing it. In a Christian's walk with the Lord, practicing hospitality reflects God's love and grace. However, in today's world, self-centered living and a lack of hospitality are common, making it essential for Christians to rediscover and uphold this Biblical principle.

Hospitality starts with understanding that it is a command from God. The Bible consistently emphasizes the importance of welcoming and caring for others. Romans 12:13 says, "Distributing to the necessity of saints; given to hospitality." This verse encourages believers to share with those in need and to be hospitable. Hospitality is more than just being polite; it is about opening our homes and hearts to others, providing for their needs, and showing them the love of Christ.

The story of Abraham in Genesis 18:1-8 is a powerful example of hospitality. When three visitors came to Abraham's tent, he hurried to welcome them, provided water to wash their feet, and prepared a meal for them. Little did he know, these visitors were angels, and one of them was the Lord Himself. This encounter not only demonstrated Abraham's hospitality but also brought him the promise of a son, showing how God blesses those who are hospitable.

Jesus Himself modeled hospitality during His ministry. He often dined with tax collectors, sinners, and those marginalized by society, showing them love and acceptance. In Luke 19:1-10, Jesus visits Zacchaeus, a tax collector, and declares that salvation has come to his house. By accepting Zacchaeus's hospitality, Jesus transformed his life.

This teaches us that hospitality can be a powerful tool for ministry, breaking down barriers and opening hearts to the gospel.

Hospitality also involves caring for those who are different from us. The parable of the Good Samaritan in Luke 10:25-37 illustrates this beautifully. When a man was beaten and left for dead, it was the Samaritan, a foreigner, who showed him compassion and took care of his needs. Jesus used this parable to teach that our neighbor is anyone in need, regardless of their background. This challenges us to extend hospitality to everyone, not just those who are like us or within our comfort zone.

In today's society, self-centered living often takes precedence over hospitality. Many people are focused on their own needs and desires, neglecting the importance of caring for others. This attitude is contrary to the teachings of the Bible. Philippians 2:3-4 says, "Let nothing be done through strife or vainglory; but in lowliness of mind let each esteem other better than themselves. Look not every man on his own things, but every man also on the things of others." As Christians, we are called to put others' needs before our own and to show hospitality as an expression of God's love.

Practicing hospitality can have a significant impact on our communities and the world. When we open our homes and hearts to others, we create opportunities for meaningful connections and demonstrate the love of Christ. This can lead to transformed lives and stronger communities. Matthew 25:35-40 underscores the importance of hospitality, as Jesus says, "For I was an hungred, and ye gave me meat: I was thirsty, and ye gave me drink: I was a stranger, and ye took me in: Naked, and ye clothed me: I was sick, and ye visited me: I was in prison, and ye came unto me. Then shall the righteous answer him, saying, Lord, when saw we thee an hungred, and fed thee? or thirsty, and gave thee drink? When saw we thee a stranger, and took thee in? or naked, and clothed thee? Or when saw we thee sick, or in prison, and came unto thee? And the King shall answer and say unto them, Verily I say unto you, Inasmuch as ye have done it unto one of the least of these my brethren, ye have done it unto me." This passage teaches that by serving others, we are serving Christ Himself.

Hospitality is also about creating an environment of welcome and inclusion within the church. Romans 15:7 says, "Wherefore receive ye one another, as Christ also received us to the glory of God." The church should be a place where everyone feels welcomed and valued. This means being intentional about greeting newcomers, making them feel at home, and including them in the life of the church. By doing so, we reflect the welcoming nature of Christ and build a strong, supportive community.

Prayer is an essential aspect of practicing hospitality. We should pray for a heart that is willing to serve others and for opportunities to show hospitality. 1 Peter 4:9-10 says, "Use hospitality one to another without grudging. As every man hath received the gift, even so minister the same one to another, as good stewards of the manifold grace of God." By seeking God's guidance and strength, we can overcome any reluctance or selfishness and be joyful in our service to others.

Hospitality also involves being generous with our resources. 2 Corinthians 9:6-7 encourages, "But this I say, He which soweth sparingly shall reap also sparingly; and he which soweth bountifully shall reap also bountifully. Every man according as he purposeth in his heart, so let him give; not grudgingly, or of necessity: for God loveth a cheerful giver." Sharing our time, money, and possessions with others is a tangible way to show hospitality and reflect God's generosity.

Teaching the next generation about the importance of hospitality is also vital. Proverbs 22:6 advises, "Train up a child in the way he should go: and when he is old, he will not depart from it." By modeling and teaching hospitality to children and young people, we help them develop a heart for serving others and instill values that will guide them throughout their lives. This can include involving them in acts of service, encouraging them to welcome others, and showing them the joy that comes from helping those in need.

The church community plays a crucial role in promoting hospitality among its members. Hebrews 10:24-25 says, "And let us consider one another to provoke unto love and to good works: Not forsaking the assembling of ourselves together, as the manner of some is; but exhorting one another: and so much the more, as ye see the day approaching." By encouraging and supporting one another, Christians can help each other stay committed to practicing hospitality. The church can provide opportunities for service, create welcoming environments, and teach about the importance of hospitality.

Hospitality can also be a powerful tool for evangelism. By opening our homes and lives to others, we create opportunities to share the gospel and demonstrate the love of Christ in practical ways. Acts 2:46-47 describes the early church's practice of hospitality: "And they, continuing daily with one accord in the temple, and breaking bread from house to house, did eat their meat with gladness and singleness of heart, Praising God, and having favour with all the people. And the Lord added to the church daily such as should be saved." Their hospitality and communal living were attractive to others and led to the growth of the church.

Moreover, hospitality is about showing kindness and compassion to those who are marginalized or in need. James 1:27 says, "Pure religion and undefiled before God and the Father is this, To visit the fatherless and widows in their affliction, and to keep himself unspotted from the world." By caring for those who are vulnerable, we reflect God's heart and fulfill His commandments. This can include visiting the sick, providing for the poor, and offering support to those who are going through difficult times.

Hospitality also involves being intentional about building relationships with others. This means taking the time to get to know people, listening to their stories, and sharing our lives with them.

Proverbs 27:17 says, "Iron sharpeneth iron; so a man sharpeneth the countenance of his friend." Building strong relationships helps us support one another, grow in our faith, and create a sense of community.

In today's fast-paced world, practicing hospitality can be challenging. Many people are busy with their own lives and may feel they do not have the time or resources to be hospitable. However, the Bible teaches that hospitality is an essential part of the Christian life. Galatians 6:9 encourages, "And let us not be weary in well doing: for in due season we shall reap, if we faint not." By prioritizing hospitality and making it a regular part of our lives, we can experience the blessings that come from serving others.

In conclusion, hospitality is a vital principle in the Bible that emphasizes the importance of welcoming and caring for others. Hebrews 13:2 teaches us to entertain strangers, as we might be serving angels unaware. Despite the trend towards self-centered living and a lack of hospitality in today's world, Christians are called to practice hospitality as an expression of God's love. This involves opening our homes and hearts to others, providing for their needs, and creating an environment of welcome and inclusion. By doing so, we reflect Christ's love, build stronger communities, and set a powerful example for others. Through prayer, generosity, and teaching the next generation, Christians can uphold the principle of hospitality and experience the blessings that come from serving others. This commitment to hospitality not only honors God but also has the potential to transform lives and communities for His glory.

Chapter 13 - Forgiveness

Forgiveness is a core principle in the Christian faith, emphasizing the need to show kindness, tenderheartedness, and forgiveness to others just as God has forgiven us through Christ. Ephesians 4:32 says, "And be ye kind one to another, tenderhearted, forgiving one another, even as God for Christ's sake hath forgiven you." This verse teaches that forgiveness is an essential part of our walk with the Lord, reflecting God's grace and mercy. However, in today's world, there is a tendency to harbor grudges and promote revenge, which is contrary to Biblical teachings. Christians are called to practice forgiveness, which not only honors God but also brings healing and restoration to relationships.

Forgiveness begins with understanding the magnitude of God's forgiveness toward us. Romans 3:23 reminds us, "For all have sinned, and come short of the glory of God." Despite our sins, God, in His great love and mercy, chose to forgive us through the sacrifice of His Son, Jesus Christ. Romans 5:8 says, "But God commendeth his love toward us, in that, while we were yet sinners, Christ died for us." This incredible act of grace sets the standard for how we are to forgive others. Since God has forgiven us so generously, we are called to extend the same forgiveness to those who wrong us.

Forgiving others is not always easy, especially when we have been deeply hurt. However, the Bible consistently teaches the importance of forgiveness. In Matthew 18:21-22, Peter asked Jesus how many times he should forgive someone who sins against him, suggesting seven times. Jesus replied, "I say not unto thee, Until seven times: but, Until seventy times seven." This response indicates that forgiveness should be limitless, reflecting God's infinite grace towards us. Holding onto grudges and seeking revenge only leads to bitterness and further conflict. Colossians 3:13 encourages, "Forbearing one another, and forgiving one another, if any man have a quarrel against any: even as Christ forgave you, so also do ye."

One powerful example of forgiveness in the Bible is the story of Joseph. His brothers sold him into slavery out of jealousy, and he endured many hardships as a result. However, when he eventually rose to a position of power in Egypt and his brothers came to him in need, Joseph chose to forgive them. In Genesis 50:20, Joseph said, "But as for you, ye thought evil against me; but God meant it unto good, to bring to pass, as it is this day, to save much people alive." Joseph's forgiveness not only restored his relationship with his brothers but also allowed God's greater plan to unfold. This story teaches us that forgiveness can lead to reconciliation and the fulfillment of God's purposes.

Forgiveness also brings personal healing and freedom. Holding onto grudges and bitterness can weigh heavily on our hearts and minds, affecting our emotional and physical health. Proverbs 17:22 says, "A merry heart doeth good like a medicine: but a broken spirit drieth the bones." By choosing to forgive, we release the burden of anger and resentment, allowing ourselves to experience peace and joy. Forgiveness frees us from the past and enables us to move forward with a lighter heart.

Furthermore, forgiveness is essential for maintaining healthy relationships. Ephesians 4:31-32 instructs, "Let all bitterness, and wrath, and anger, and clamour, and evil speaking, be put away from you, with all malice: And be ye kind one to another, tenderhearted, forgiving one another, even as God for Christ's sake hath forgiven you." Kindness and tenderheartedness are crucial for fostering love and understanding in our interactions with others. When we forgive, we demonstrate humility and compassion, which strengthen our relationships and reflect Christ's love.

In addition to personal relationships, forgiveness is vital for the unity and health of the church. Colossians 3:12-14 says, "Put on therefore, as the elect of God, holy and beloved, bowels of mercies, kindness, humbleness of mind, meekness, longsuffering; Forbearing one another, and forgiving one another, if any man have a quarrel against any: even as Christ forgave you, so also do ye. And above all these things put on charity, which is the bond of perfectness." The church is called to be a community of love and forgiveness, where members support and care for one another. By practicing forgiveness, we maintain unity and create a welcoming environment where God's love can flourish.

Forgiveness also has a powerful impact on our witness to the world. In John 13:34-35, Jesus said, "A new commandment I give unto you, That ye love one another; as I have loved you, that ye also love one another. By this shall all men know that ye are my disciples, if ye have love one to another." Our willingness to forgive and love others sets us apart and demonstrates the transformative power of God's grace. When others see our forgiveness, they are more likely to be drawn to the gospel and experience God's love for themselves.

Prayer is an essential part of practicing forgiveness. In the Lord's Prayer, Jesus taught us to pray, "And forgive us our debts, as we forgive our debtors" (Matthew 6:12). This prayer reminds us of our need for God's forgiveness and our responsibility to forgive others. By seeking God's help and strength, we can overcome the natural inclination to hold grudges and seek revenge. Philippians 4:13 assures us, "I can do all things through Christ which strengtheneth me." Through prayer and reliance on God's power, we can extend forgiveness even in the most challenging situations.

Teaching the next generation about forgiveness is also crucial. Proverbs 22:6 advises, "Train up a child in the way he should go: and when he is old, he will not depart from it." By modeling and teaching forgiveness to children and young people, we help them develop a heart of compassion and grace. This can include encouraging them to resolve conflicts peacefully, apologizing when they are wrong, and extending forgiveness to others. Teaching forgiveness prepares them to navigate relationships with love and understanding throughout their lives.

The church community plays a vital role in promoting forgiveness among its members. Hebrews 10:24-25 says, "And let us consider one another to provoke unto love and to good works: Not forsaking the assembling of ourselves together, as the manner of some is; but exhorting one another: and so much the more, as ye see the day approaching." By encouraging and supporting one another, Christians can help each other stay committed to practicing forgiveness. The church can provide teaching, resources, and opportunities for reconciliation, fostering a culture of grace and forgiveness.

Forgiveness also involves setting healthy boundaries and seeking justice when necessary. Forgiving someone does not mean allowing them to continue harmful behavior. Matthew 18:15-17 provides a process for addressing sin within the church, emphasizing the importance of confronting wrongdoing and seeking reconciliation. By setting boundaries and seeking justice, we protect ourselves and others while still extending forgiveness and grace.

In conclusion, forgiveness is a fundamental principle in the Christian faith, reflecting the kindness, tenderheartedness, and forgiveness that God has shown us through Christ. Ephesians 4:32 teaches us to be kind and forgiving, just as God has forgiven us. Despite the tendency to harbor grudges and promote revenge in today's world, Christians are called to practice forgiveness as an expression of God's love and grace. This involves understanding the magnitude of God's forgiveness, choosing to forgive even when it is difficult, and seeking reconciliation and healing in relationships. By practicing forgiveness, we experience personal freedom and peace, maintain healthy relationships, and create a welcoming and unified church community. Through prayer, teaching the next generation, and supporting one another, Christians can uphold the principle of forgiveness and reflect God's love to the world. This commitment to forgiveness not only honors God but also transforms lives and relationships for His glory.

Chapter 14 - Faithfulness

Faithfulness is a cornerstone of the Christian faith, emphasizing steadfast loyalty, trustworthiness, and reliability in all aspects of life. Proverbs 3:3 says, "Let not mercy and truth forsake thee: bind them about thy neck; write them upon the table of thine heart." This verse teaches that mercy and truth, which are integral to faithfulness, should be deeply embedded in our lives. In today's world, infidelity and broken promises are common, attacking the very essence of faithfulness. As Christians, we are called to uphold the principles of faithfulness in our walk with the Lord, reflecting God's unwavering faithfulness to us and maintaining integrity in our relationships and commitments.

Faithfulness begins with understanding God's faithfulness towards us. Lamentations 3:22-23 reminds us, "It is of the Lord's mercies that we are not consumed, because his compassions fail not. They are new every morning: great is thy faithfulness." God's faithfulness is constant and unfailing, providing a perfect example for us to follow. He keeps His promises and remains steadfast in His love and mercy toward us. This assurance of God's faithfulness gives us confidence and security, enabling us to be faithful in our own lives.

One of the key areas where faithfulness is essential is in our relationship with God. Deuteronomy 6:5 says, "And thou shalt love the Lord thy God with all thine heart, and with all thy soul, and with all thy might." Our devotion to God should be unwavering, reflecting complete loyalty and trust in Him. This means consistently spending time in prayer, studying His Word, and living according to His commandments. By being faithful to God, we strengthen our relationship with Him and grow in our spiritual journey.

Faithfulness is also vital in our relationships with others. In marriage, faithfulness is the foundation of trust and love. Hebrews 13:4 states, "Marriage is honourable in all, and the bed undefiled: but whoremongers and adulterers God will judge." Infidelity not only breaks the trust between spouses but also dishonors God. Ephesians 5:25-28 provides a beautiful picture of marital faithfulness: "Husbands, love your wives, even as Christ also loved the church, and gave himself for it; That he might sanctify and cleanse it with the washing of water by the word, That he might present it to himself a glorious church, not having spot, or wrinkle, or any such thing; but that it should be holy and without blemish. So ought men to love their wives as their own bodies. He that loveth his wife loveth himself." This passage teaches that marital faithfulness involves selfless love, care, and devotion, mirroring Christ's love for the church.

Faithfulness extends beyond marriage to all relationships, including friendships, family, and the church community. Proverbs 17:17 says, "A friend loveth at all times, and a brother is born for adversity." Being a faithful friend means being reliable, supportive, and trustworthy, especially during difficult times. Faithfulness in relationships builds strong, lasting bonds and reflects God's love to others. It means keeping promises, being dependable, and standing by others through thick and thin.

In the church community, faithfulness is crucial for maintaining unity and harmony. 1 Corinthians 4:2 says, "Moreover it is required in stewards, that a man be found faithful." Church members are stewards of God's work and should be faithful in their service, attendance, and support of one another. By being faithful, we contribute to a thriving, supportive, and loving church environment where everyone can grow in their faith.

Faithfulness is also important in our work and daily responsibilities. Colossians 3:23-24 instructs, "And whatsoever ye do, do it heartily, as to the Lord, and not unto men; Knowing that of the Lord ye shall receive the reward of the inheritance: for ye serve the Lord Christ." Working diligently and with integrity reflects our faithfulness to God and sets a positive example for others. Whether in our jobs, studies, or volunteer work, being reliable and committed honors God and demonstrates our dedication.

Broken promises are a significant issue in today's society, undermining trust and integrity. Matthew 5:37 says, "But let your communication be, Yea, yea; Nay, nay: for whatsoever is more than these cometh of evil." This verse teaches the importance of keeping our word and being honest in our commitments. By following through on our promises, we build trust and credibility in our relationships. This applies to all areas of life, including our personal, professional, and spiritual commitments.

Prayer is a vital aspect of maintaining faithfulness. By seeking God's guidance and strength, we can remain steadfast in our commitments and overcome the temptations that lead to infidelity and broken promises. Philippians 4:6-7 encourages, "Be careful for nothing; but in every thing by prayer and supplication with thanksgiving let your requests be made known unto God. And the peace of God, which passeth all understanding, shall keep your hearts and minds through Christ Jesus." Through prayer, we can stay connected to God, draw on His strength, and receive the peace that enables us to be faithful.

Teaching the next generation about faithfulness is also crucial. Proverbs 22:6 advises, "Train up a child in the way he should go: and when he is old, he will not depart from it." By modeling and teaching faithfulness to children and young people, we help them develop strong moral values and a commitment to integrity. This includes teaching them the importance of keeping their promises, being reliable, and standing by their commitments. By instilling these values early on, we prepare them to live faithfully in their personal and professional lives.

The church community plays a significant role in promoting faithfulness among its members. Hebrews 10:24-25 says, "And let us consider one another to provoke unto love and to good works: Not forsaking the assembling of ourselves together, as the manner of some is; but exhorting one another: and so much the more, as ye see the day approaching." By encouraging and supporting one another, Christians can help each other stay committed to living faithfully. The church can provide teaching, resources, and opportunities for accountability, fostering a culture of faithfulness.

Faithfulness also involves being good stewards of the resources and opportunities God has given us. Luke 16:10 says, "He that is faithful in that which is least is faithful also in much: and he that is unjust in the least is unjust also in much." By being faithful with what we have, whether it is our time, talents, or possessions, we honor God and demonstrate our trustworthiness. This includes using our resources wisely, giving generously, and serving others faithfully.

In conclusion, faithfulness is a fundamental principle in the Christian faith, emphasizing steadfast loyalty, trustworthiness, and reliability. Proverbs 3:3 teaches us to bind mercy and truth about our necks and write them on the table of our hearts, reflecting faithfulness in all aspects of our lives. Despite the prevalence of infidelity and broken promises in today's world, Christians are called to uphold the principles of faithfulness. This involves being faithful to God, maintaining integrity in our relationships, keeping our promises, and being reliable in our work and daily responsibilities. By seeking God's guidance through prayer, teaching the next generation, and supporting one another within the church community, we can live faithfully and reflect God's unwavering faithfulness to the world. This commitment to faithfulness not only honors God but also strengthens our relationships, builds trust, and creates a positive and supportive community for His glory. Through our faithfulness, we demonstrate the love and grace of God, making a lasting impact on those around us.

Chapter 15 - Modesty

Modesty is a significant principle in the Christian faith, emphasizing humility, decency, and respect in behavior and appearance. 1 Timothy 2:9 says, "In like manner also, that women adorn themselves in modest apparel, with shamefacedness and sobriety; not with broided hair, or gold, or pearls, or costly array." This verse teaches that modesty should be reflected in how we dress and present ourselves, avoiding excessive adornment and focusing on inner beauty and godliness. In today's world, there is a widespread promotion of immodesty and provocative behavior, which undermines the values of modesty and decency. As Christians, it is essential to uphold the principles of modesty in our walk with the Lord, reflecting our commitment to honoring God and respecting ourselves and others.

Modesty begins with understanding that our bodies are temples of the Holy Spirit. 1 Corinthians 6:19-20 reminds us, "What? know ye not that your body is the temple of the Holy Ghost which is in you, which ye have of God, and ye are not your own? For ye are bought with a price: therefore glorify God in your body, and in your spirit, which are God's." This verse teaches that our bodies belong to God, and we should use them to glorify Him. This includes dressing and behaving in ways that reflect His holiness and purity.

One aspect of modesty is dressing appropriately and avoiding clothing that is revealing or provocative. 1 Timothy 2:9 emphasizes modest apparel, shamefacedness, and sobriety. Modest clothing is not about following strict rules or being unattractive; it is about honoring God and respecting ourselves and others. By choosing modest clothing, we demonstrate our commitment to purity and decency, avoiding the temptation to draw inappropriate attention to ourselves. Modesty also involves our behavior and attitudes. 1 Peter 3:3-4 says, "Whose adorning let it not be that outward adorning of plaiting the hair, and of wearing of gold, or of putting on of apparel; But let it be the hidden man of the heart, in that which is not corruptible, even the ornament of a meek and quiet spirit, which is in the sight of God of great price." This verse teaches that true beauty comes from within, from a meek and quiet spirit that reflects God's character. Modest behavior includes humility, gentleness, and self-control, avoiding boastfulness, arrogance, and provocative actions.

In contrast, today's culture often promotes immodesty and provocative behavior, encouraging people to seek attention through their appearance and actions. This is evident in the media, fashion industry, and social norms, where immodesty is often glamorized and celebrated. As Christians, we are called to be different from the world and to uphold God's standards of modesty and decency. Romans 12:2 instructs, "And be not conformed to this world: but be ye transformed by the renewing of your mind, that ye may prove what is that good, and acceptable, and perfect, will of God." By renewing our minds with God's Word and seeking His guidance, we can resist the pressures to conform to the world's standards and live according to His principles.

Modesty is also about respecting others and not causing them to stumble. Romans 14:13 says, "Let us not therefore judge one another any more: but judge this rather, that no man put a stumblingblock or an occasion to fall in his brother's way." By dressing and behaving modestly, we avoid causing others to stumble into temptation or sin. This reflects our love and consideration for others, seeking to build them up rather than leading them astray.

Prayer is a vital aspect of maintaining modesty. By seeking God's help and strength, we can develop a heart of modesty and purity. Philippians 4:6-7 encourages, "Be careful for nothing; but in every thing by prayer and supplication with thanksgiving let your requests be made known unto God. And the peace of God, which passeth all understanding, shall keep your hearts and minds through Christ Jesus." Through prayer, we can stay connected to God, draw on His strength, and receive the peace that enables us to live modestly.

Teaching the next generation about modesty is also crucial. Proverbs 22:6 advises, "Train up a child in the way he should go: and when he is old, he will not depart from it." By modeling and teaching modesty to children and young people, we help them develop strong moral values and a commitment to purity and decency. This includes teaching them the importance of dressing appropriately, behaving respectfully, and valuing inner beauty over outward appearance. By instilling these values early on, we prepare them to live modestly in their personal and social lives.

The church community plays a significant role in promoting modesty among its members. Hebrews 10:24-25 says, "And let us consider one another to provoke unto love and to good works: Not forsaking the assembling of ourselves together, as the manner of some is; but exhorting one another: and so much the more, as ye see the day approaching." By encouraging and supporting one another, Christians can help each other stay committed to living modestly. The church can provide teaching, resources, and opportunities for accountability, fostering a culture of modesty and decency.

Modesty is also about focusing on our inner beauty and character. 1 Samuel 16:7 reminds us, "But the Lord said unto Samuel, Look not on his countenance, or on the height of his stature; because I have refused him: for the Lord seeth not as man seeth; for man looketh on the outward appearance, but the Lord looketh on the heart." God values our hearts and character more than our outward appearance. By prioritizing inner beauty and developing qualities such as humility, kindness, and self-control, we reflect God's character and honor Him in our lives.

In conclusion, modesty is a fundamental principle in the Christian faith, emphasizing humility, decency, and respect in behavior and appearance. 1 Timothy 2:9 teaches that modesty should be reflected in how we dress and present ourselves, avoiding excessive adornment and focusing on inner beauty and godliness. Despite the promotion of immodesty and provocative behavior in today's world, Christians are called to uphold the principles of modesty. This involves dressing appropriately, behaving respectfully, and valuing inner beauty over outward appearance. By seeking God's guidance through prayer, teaching the next generation, and supporting one another within the church community, we can live modestly and reflect God's holiness and purity. This commitment to modesty not only honors God but also protects ourselves and others from temptation and sin, creating a positive and supportive environment for His glory. Through our modesty, we demonstrate the love and grace of God, making a lasting impact on those around us.

Chapter 16 - Love and Sacrifice

Love and sacrifice are central to the Christian faith, emphasizing the importance of putting others before ourselves and demonstrating the ultimate form of love through selflessness. John 15:13 says, "Greater love hath no man than this, that a man lay down his life for his friends." This verse highlights the profound nature of sacrificial love, which is the greatest expression of love one can show. In today's world, selfishness and a lack of sacrificial love are prevalent, often leading people away from the selfless example set by Christ. As Christians, it is essential to embody the principles of love and sacrifice in our walk with the Lord, reflecting His love and bringing His light to others.

Understanding God's love and sacrifice is the foundation for practicing it in our own lives. John 3:16 declares, "For God so loved the world, that he gave his only begotten Son, that whosoever believeth in him should not perish, but have everlasting life." This verse shows the magnitude of God's love for humanity, willing to sacrifice His only Son for our salvation. Jesus' sacrifice on the cross is the ultimate act of love, offering Himself to atone for our sins and reconcile us with God. This sacrificial love sets the standard for how we are to love others.

Christians are called to love one another just as Christ loves us. John 13:34-35 instructs, "A new commandment I give unto you, That ye love one another; as I have loved you, that ye also love one another. By this shall all men know that ye are my disciples, if ye have love one to another." Our love for others should be characterized by selflessness, compassion, and a willingness to put their needs before our own. This kind of love is not based on feelings or emotions but on a deliberate choice to act in the best interest of others.

Sacrificial love involves giving up our own desires and comforts for the sake of others. Philippians 2:3-4 teaches, "Let nothing be done through strife or vainglory; but in lowliness of mind let each esteem other better than themselves. Look not every man on his own things, but every man also on the things of others." This passage calls us to humility and selflessness, considering others' needs above our own. By doing so, we follow Christ's example, who humbled Himself and became a servant to all.

One of the most powerful examples of love and sacrifice in the Bible is the story of the Good Samaritan. In Luke 10:30-37, Jesus tells the parable of a man who was beaten and left for dead. While a priest and a Levite passed by without helping, a Samaritan stopped, cared for the man's wounds, and provided for his needs. This Samaritan's actions exemplify sacrificial love, as he put aside his own plans and resources to help a stranger. Jesus concludes the parable by instructing us to "Go, and do thou likewise." This story challenges us to show love and compassion to those in need, even if it requires personal sacrifice.

Selfishness, on the other hand, is a significant barrier to practicing sacrificial love. 1 Corinthians 13:4-5 describes love in this way: "Charity suffereth long, and is kind; charity envieth not; charity vaunteth not itself, is not puffed up, Doth not behave itself unseemly, seeketh not her own, is not easily provoked, thinketh no evil." True love is patient, kind, and selfless. It does not seek its own benefit but seeks the good of others. By overcoming selfishness, we can demonstrate genuine love that reflects the heart of Christ.

Prayer is an essential aspect of developing a heart of love and sacrifice. By seeking God's help and strength, we can grow in our ability to love others selflessly. Philippians 4:6-7 encourages, "Be careful for nothing; but in every thing by prayer and supplication with thanksgiving let your requests be made known unto God. And the peace of God, which passeth all understanding, shall keep your hearts and minds through Christ Jesus." Through prayer, we can stay connected to God, draw on His strength, and receive the peace that enables us to love sacrificially.

Teaching the next generation about love and sacrifice is also crucial. Proverbs 22:6 advises, "Train up a child in the way he should go: and when he is old, he will not depart from it." By modeling and teaching sacrificial love to children and young people, we help them develop strong moral values and a commitment to selflessness. This includes encouraging them to share, help others, and put others' needs before their own. By instilling these values early on, we prepare them to live lives of love and sacrifice.

The church community plays a significant role in promoting love and sacrifice among its members. Hebrews 10:24-25 says, "And let us consider one another to provoke unto love and to good works: Not forsaking the assembling of ourselves together, as the manner of some is; but exhorting one another: and so much the more, as ye see the day approaching." By encouraging and supporting one another, Christians can help each other stay committed to living lives of love and sacrifice. The church can provide teaching, resources, and opportunities for service, fostering a culture of selflessness and compassion.

Love and sacrifice also involve forgiving others. Ephesians 4:32 instructs, "And be ye kind one to another, tenderhearted, forgiving one another, even as God for Christ's sake hath forgiven you." Forgiveness is a significant aspect of sacrificial love, requiring us to let go of grudges and extend grace to those who have wronged us. By forgiving others, we reflect the forgiveness we have received from God and demonstrate His love to the world.

In addition to personal relationships, love and sacrifice extend to serving our communities and those in need. Matthew 25:35-40 emphasizes the importance of serving others: "For I was an hungred, and ye gave me meat: I was thirsty, and ye gave me drink: I was a stranger, and ye took me in: Naked, and ye clothed me: I was sick, and ye visited me: I was in prison, and ye came unto me. Then shall the righteous answer him, saying, Lord, when saw we thee an hungred, and fed thee? or thirsty, and gave thee drink? When saw we thee a stranger, and took thee in? or naked, and clothed thee? Or when saw we thee sick, or in prison, and came unto thee? And the King shall answer and say unto them, Verily I say unto you, Inasmuch as ye have done it unto one of the least of these my brethren, ye have done it unto me." This passage teaches that by serving those in need, we serve Christ Himself. Our love and sacrifice should be evident in our actions toward those who are less fortunate.

Moreover, love and sacrifice involve sharing the gospel and making disciples. The Great Commission in Matthew 28:19-20 instructs, "Go ye therefore, and teach all nations, baptizing them in the name of the Father, and of the Son, and of the Holy Ghost: Teaching them to observe all things whatsoever I have commanded you: and, lo, I am with you alway, even unto the end of the world. Amen." Sharing the good news of Jesus Christ is an act of love, as it offers others the hope and salvation that we have received. It requires sacrifice, as it may involve stepping out of our comfort zones, facing rejection, or giving our time and resources.

Love and sacrifice also require us to stand up for justice and righteousness. Micah 6:8 says, "He hath shewed thee, O man, what is good; and what doth the Lord require of thee, but to do justly, and to love mercy, and to walk humbly with thy God?" As Christians, we are called to advocate for justice and show mercy to those who are oppressed or marginalized. This may involve speaking out against injustice, supporting those who are suffering, and working towards creating a fair and just society.

In conclusion, love and sacrifice are fundamental principles in the Christian faith, emphasizing selflessness, compassion, and the willingness to put others before ourselves. John 15:13 teaches that the greatest form of love is to lay down one's life for one's friends, reflecting the sacrificial love of Christ. Despite the prevalence of selfishness and a lack of sacrificial love in today's world, Christians are called to embody these principles in their walk with the Lord. This involves understanding God's love and sacrifice, loving others selflessly, serving those in need, sharing the gospel, and standing up for justice and righteousness. By seeking God's guidance through prayer, teaching the next generation, and supporting one another within the church community, we can live lives of love and sacrifice that honor God and reflect His love to the world. This commitment to love and sacrifice not only strengthens our relationships and communities but also makes a lasting impact on those around us, bringing glory to God. Through our love and sacrifice, we demonstrate the heart of Christ and fulfill His command to love one another as He has loved us.

Chapter 17 - Discipline

Discipline is a crucial aspect of the Christian life, emphasizing the need for correction, self-control, and adherence to God's principles. Proverbs 13:24 says, "He that spareth his rod hateth his son: but he that loveth him chasteneth him betimes." This verse highlights the importance of discipline in showing love and guiding others toward righteousness. In today's world, permissive parenting and a lack of discipline are prevalent, undermining the values of self-control and responsibility. As Christians, it is essential to understand and practice discipline in our walk with the Lord, reflecting God's love and maintaining order and righteousness in our lives and relationships.

Discipline begins with recognizing its role in God's character and His relationship with us. Hebrews 12:6 says, "For whom the Lord loveth he chasteneth, and scourgeth every son whom he receiveth." This verse teaches that God's discipline is a sign of His love and care for us. Just as a loving parent disciplines their child to teach and protect them, God disciplines us to guide us in His ways and help us grow spiritually. Understanding that discipline is an expression of God's love helps us accept and appreciate it in our lives.

One aspect of discipline is self-control, which is essential for living a godly life. Galatians 5:22-23 lists self-control as one of the fruits of the Spirit: "But the fruit of the Spirit is love, joy, peace, longsuffering, gentleness, goodness, faith, Meekness, temperance: against such there is no law." Self-control involves managing our desires, emotions, and actions in accordance with God's will. It means resisting temptation, making wise choices, and prioritizing our spiritual growth. By practicing self-control, we reflect God's character and maintain a life that honors Him.

Discipline also involves correction and instruction, which are vital for personal and spiritual growth. Proverbs 3:11-12 advises, "My son, despise not the chastening of the Lord; neither be weary of his correction: For whom the Lord loveth he correcteth; even as a father the son in whom he delighteth." Accepting correction helps us learn from our mistakes and align our lives with God's principles. This can come through God's Word, the guidance of the Holy Spirit, or the counsel of others. By being open to correction, we demonstrate humility and a desire to grow in righteousness.

In the context of parenting, discipline is essential for teaching children right from wrong and guiding them in the ways of the Lord. Proverbs 22:6 says, "Train up a child in the way he should go: and when he is old, he will not depart from it." Permissive parenting, which avoids discipline, fails to provide the necessary boundaries and guidance children need. Ephesians 6:4 instructs, "And, ye fathers, provoke not your children to wrath: but bring them up in the nurture and admonition of the Lord." By disciplining children lovingly and consistently, parents help them develop self-control, respect for authority, and a strong moral foundation.

Discipline is also important in maintaining order and harmony within the church community. 1 Corinthians 14:40 says, "Let all things be done decently and in order." The church should be a place of order, where members respect and follow the principles set forth in God's Word. This includes addressing sin within the community and encouraging one another to live according to God's standards. Matthew 18:15-17 provides a process for church discipline, emphasizing the importance of addressing sin and seeking reconciliation: "Moreover if thy brother shall trespass against thee, go and tell him his fault between thee and him alone: if he shall hear thee, thou hast gained thy brother. But if he will not hear thee, then take with thee one or two more, that in the mouth of two or three witnesses every word may be established. And if he shall neglect to hear them, tell it unto the church: but if he neglect to hear the church, let him be unto thee as an heathen man and a publican." This process aims to restore relationships and maintain the purity of the church.

Prayer is an essential part of developing discipline in our lives. By seeking God's guidance and strength, we can grow in self-control and the ability to accept correction. Philippians 4:6-7 encourages, "Be careful for nothing; but in every thing by prayer and supplication with thanksgiving let your requests be made known unto God. And the peace of God, which passeth all understanding, shall keep your hearts and minds through Christ Jesus." Through prayer, we can stay connected to God, draw on His strength, and receive the peace that enables us to live disciplined lives.

Teaching the next generation about discipline is also crucial. Proverbs 29:17 advises, "Correct thy son, and he shall give thee rest; yea, he shall give delight unto thy soul." By modeling and teaching discipline to children and young people, we help them develop strong moral values and a commitment to self-control and responsibility. This includes setting boundaries, providing consistent guidance, and encouraging them to make wise choices. By instilling these values early on, we prepare them to live disciplined lives that honor God.

The church community plays a significant role in promoting discipline among its members. Hebrews 10:24-25 says, "And let us consider one another to provoke unto love and to good works: Not forsaking the assembling of ourselves together, as the manner of some is; but exhorting one another: and so much the more, as ye see the day approaching." By encouraging and supporting one another, Christians can help each other stay committed to living disciplined lives. The church can provide teaching, resources, and opportunities for accountability, fostering a culture of discipline and order.

Discipline is also about setting and maintaining boundaries in our lives. Proverbs 25:28 says, "He that hath no rule over his own spirit is like a city that is broken down, and without walls." Setting boundaries helps us protect ourselves from temptation and maintain focus on our spiritual goals. This includes managing our time, avoiding harmful influences, and prioritizing our relationship with God. By establishing and maintaining boundaries, we create an environment that supports our spiritual growth and honors God.

Discipline extends to our work and daily responsibilities as well. Colossians 3:23-24 instructs, "And whatsoever ye do, do it heartily, as to the Lord, and not unto men; Knowing that of the Lord ye shall receive the reward of the inheritance: for ye serve the Lord Christ." Working diligently and with integrity reflects our discipline and commitment to God. Whether in our jobs, studies, or volunteer work, being reliable and responsible honors God and sets a positive example for others.

In addition to personal discipline, we are called to help others grow in discipline. Galatians 6:1 says, "Brethren, if a man be overtaken in a fault, ye which are spiritual, restore such an one in the spirit of meekness; considering thyself, lest thou also be tempted." By gently correcting and encouraging one another, we help each other stay on the path of righteousness. This involves being patient, understanding, and supportive, recognizing that we all need help and accountability in our spiritual journey.

Discipline is also about persevering through challenges and hardships. James 1:2-4 teaches, "My brethren, count it all joy when ye fall into divers temptations; Knowing this, that the trying of your faith worketh patience. But let patience have her perfect work, that ye may be perfect and entire, wanting nothing." Facing difficulties with perseverance and discipline helps us grow stronger in our faith and develop a deeper reliance on God. By trusting in God's plan and maintaining discipline, we can navigate life's challenges and emerge more resilient and faithful.

In conclusion, discipline is a fundamental principle in the Christian faith, emphasizing correction, self-control, and adherence to God's principles. Proverbs 13:24 teaches that discipline is an expression of love, guiding others toward righteousness. Despite the prevalence of permissive parenting and a lack of discipline in today's world,

Christians are called to uphold the principles of discipline. This involves practicing self-control, accepting correction, setting boundaries, and persevering through challenges. By seeking God's guidance through prayer, teaching the next generation, and supporting one another within the church community, we can live disciplined lives that honor God. This commitment to discipline not only strengthens our relationships and communities but also reflects God's character and brings glory to Him. Through our discipline, we demonstrate the love and grace of God, making a lasting impact on those around us.

Chapter 18 - Humility

Humility is a fundamental principle in the Christian faith, emphasizing the importance of putting others before ourselves and recognizing our dependence on God. Philippians 2:3 says, "Let nothing be done through strife or vainglory; but in lowliness of mind let each esteem other better than themselves." This verse teaches that humility involves setting aside selfish ambition and pride, and instead, valuing others above ourselves. In today's world, pride and arrogance are often promoted, leading people away from the humility that Christ exemplified. As Christians, it is essential to embody humility in our walk with the Lord, reflecting His character and fostering unity and love in our relationships.

Understanding the humility of Jesus Christ is the foundation for practicing it in our own lives. Philippians 2:5-8 says, "Let this mind be in you, which was also in Christ Jesus: Who, being in the form of God, thought it not robbery to be equal with God: But made himself of no reputation, and took upon him the form of a servant, and was made in the likeness of men: And being found in fashion as a man, he humbled himself, and became obedient unto death, even the death of the cross." Jesus, though He was God, humbled Himself by becoming a man and ultimately sacrificing His life for us. This ultimate act of humility sets the standard for how we are to live.

One aspect of humility is recognizing our dependence on God. James 4:10 says, "Humble yourselves in the sight of the Lord, and he shall lift you up." Acknowledging that we cannot achieve anything of lasting value without God helps us maintain a humble heart. This means seeking His guidance, relying on His strength, and giving Him the glory for our achievements. By doing so, we demonstrate our trust in God and our understanding of His sovereignty.

Humility also involves serving others. Jesus demonstrated this through His actions, such as washing the disciples' feet in John 13:1-17.

In verse 14-15, He says, "If I then, your Lord and Master, have washed your feet; ye also ought to wash one another's feet. For I have given you an example, that ye should do as I have done to you." Serving others, even in humble and menial ways, reflects the humility of Christ and shows our love and respect for others. This can include acts of kindness, helping those in need, and putting others' needs before our own.

Pride and arrogance are significant barriers to humility. Proverbs 16:18 warns, "Pride goeth before destruction, and an haughty spirit before a fall." Pride leads to a false sense of self-sufficiency and superiority, causing us to look down on others and neglect our dependence on God. By contrast, humility fosters genuine relationships and a healthy dependence on God. Romans 12:3 advises, "For I say, through the grace given unto me, to every man that is among you, not to think of himself more highly than he ought to think; but to think soberly, according as God hath dealt to every man the measure of faith." This verse encourages us to have a realistic and humble view of ourselves, recognizing that our abilities and gifts come from God.

Humility is also crucial for maintaining unity within the church. Ephesians 4:2-3 says, "With all lowliness and meekness, with longsuffering, forbearing one another in love; Endeavouring to keep the unity of the Spirit in the bond of peace." By practicing humility, we can foster an environment of love and cooperation, avoiding conflicts and divisions. This involves listening to others, valuing their contributions, and working together for the common good. Colossians 3:12-13 further emphasizes this: "Put on therefore, as the elect of God, holy and beloved, bowels of mercies, kindness, humbleness of mind, meekness, longsuffering; Forbearing one another, and forgiving one another, if any man have a quarrel against any: even as Christ forgave you, so also do ye." By forgiving and bearing with one another, we maintain harmony and reflect the humility of Christ.

Prayer is a vital aspect of developing humility. By seeking God's help and strength, we can overcome pride and cultivate a humble heart.

Philippians 4:6-7 encourages, "Be careful for nothing; but in every thing by prayer and supplication with thanksgiving let your requests be made known unto God. And the peace of God, which passeth all understanding, shall keep your hearts and minds through Christ Jesus." Through prayer, we can stay connected to God, draw on His strength, and receive the peace that enables us to live humbly.

Teaching the next generation about humility is also crucial. Proverbs 22:6 advises, "Train up a child in the way he should go: and when he is old, he will not depart from it." By modeling and teaching humility to children and young people, we help them develop strong moral values and a commitment to selflessness. This includes encouraging them to serve others, recognize their dependence on God, and value others above themselves. By instilling these values early on, we prepare them to live lives of humility that honor God.

The church community plays a significant role in promoting humility among its members. Hebrews 10:24-25 says, "And let us consider one another to provoke unto love and to good works: Not forsaking the assembling of ourselves together, as the manner of some is; but exhorting one another: and so much the more, as ye see the day approaching." By encouraging and supporting one another, Christians can help each other stay committed to living humbly. The church can provide teaching, resources, and opportunities for service, fostering a culture of humility and mutual respect.

Humility is also about recognizing and valuing the contributions of others. 1 Corinthians 12:25-26 says, "That there should be no schism in the body; but that the members should have the same care one for another. And whether one member suffer, all the members suffer with it; or one member be honoured, all the members rejoice with it." By valuing and honoring each other's contributions, we reflect the unity and diversity of the body of Christ. This involves appreciating the different gifts and talents that God has given to each person and working together to build up the church.

Humility extends to our interactions with the world as well. 1 Peter 3:15 says, "But sanctify the Lord God in your hearts: and be ready always to give an answer to every man that asketh you a reason of the hope that is in you with meekness and fear." By sharing our faith with humility and respect, we can effectively witness to others and reflect the love of Christ. This involves listening to others, respecting their perspectives, and sharing the gospel with gentleness and compassion.

In conclusion, humility is a fundamental principle in the Christian faith, emphasizing the importance of putting others before ourselves and recognizing our dependence on God. Philippians 2:3 teaches that humility involves setting aside selfish ambition and pride, and instead, valuing others above ourselves. Despite the prevalence of pride and arrogance in today's world, Christians are called to embody humility in their walk with the Lord. This involves recognizing our dependence on God, serving others, maintaining unity within the church, and valuing the contributions of others. By seeking God's guidance through prayer, teaching the next generation, and supporting one another within the church community, we can live lives of humility that honor God. This commitment to humility not only strengthens our relationships and communities but also reflects God's character and brings glory to Him. Through our humility, we demonstrate the love and grace of God, making a lasting impact on those around us. By following the example of Jesus Christ, who humbled Himself even to the point of death on a cross, we can cultivate a heart of humility and live lives that truly honor our Lord.

Chaptert 19 - Prayer

Prayer is a vital aspect of the Christian life, emphasizing constant communication with God and reliance on His guidance and strength. 1 Thessalonians 5:17 says, "Pray without ceasing." This verse highlights the importance of maintaining a continuous and consistent prayer life, staying connected to God in all circumstances. In today's world, many people neglect prayer and rely on their own abilities rather than depending on God. As Christians, it is essential to cultivate a strong prayer life, reflecting our dependence on the Lord and seeking His will in every aspect of our lives.

Prayer begins with understanding that it is a direct line of communication with God. Philippians 4:6-7 says, "Be careful for nothing; but in every thing by prayer and supplication with thanksgiving let your requests be made known unto God. And the peace of God, which passeth all understanding, shall keep your hearts and minds through Christ Jesus." This passage teaches that prayer is a way to bring all our concerns, needs, and gratitude before God. It is through prayer that we experience His peace, which guards our hearts and minds. By making prayer a regular part of our lives, we can stay connected to God and receive His guidance and comfort.

One aspect of prayer is acknowledging our dependence on God. Proverbs 3:5-6 instructs, "Trust in the Lord with all thine heart; and lean not unto thine own understanding. In all thy ways acknowledge him, and he shall direct thy paths." Prayer is an expression of our trust in God, recognizing that we need His wisdom and direction in all areas of our lives. When we pray, we surrender our own understanding and seek His will, trusting that He knows what is best for us. This dependence on God helps us to remain humble and focused on His plans rather than our own.

Prayer also involves seeking God's will and aligning our desires with His. In Matthew 6:10, part of the Lord's Prayer, Jesus teaches us to pray, "Thy kingdom come. Thy will be done in earth, as it is in heaven." This emphasizes the importance of desiring God's will above our own and seeking His kingdom and righteousness in our prayers. By praying for God's will to be done, we demonstrate our commitment to His purposes and our willingness to submit to His authority.

Another important aspect of prayer is interceding for others. James 5:16 says, "Confess your faults one to another, and pray one for another, that ye may be healed. The effectual fervent prayer of a righteous man availeth much." Intercessory prayer involves bringing the needs of others before God and asking for His intervention and blessings in their lives. This not only strengthens our relationships with others but also reflects our love and compassion for them. By praying for others, we participate in God's work and demonstrate our trust in His power to change lives.

Prayer also plays a crucial role in spiritual growth and transformation. Romans 12:12 encourages, "Rejoicing in hope; patient in tribulation; continuing instant in prayer." Persistent prayer helps us to remain hopeful and patient in difficult times, allowing God to work in and through us. It is through prayer that we can experience spiritual renewal, strength, and the ability to overcome challenges. By making prayer a constant practice, we open ourselves to the transforming power of the Holy Spirit.

In addition to personal prayer, corporate prayer is vital for the health and unity of the church. Acts 2:42 describes the early church: "And they continued stedfastly in the apostles' doctrine and fellowship, and in breaking of bread, and in prayers." Corporate prayer brings believers together, fostering unity and a shared sense of purpose. It allows the church to seek God's guidance collectively and support one another in their spiritual journeys. By participating in corporate prayer, we strengthen the body of Christ and experience the power of communal worship.

Despite the importance of prayer, many people neglect it, relying instead on their own strength and understanding. This neglect can lead to spiritual dryness and a lack of direction. Jesus emphasized the necessity of abiding in Him through prayer in John 15:5: "I am the vine, ye are the branches: He that abideth in me, and I in him, the same bringeth forth much fruit: for without me ye can do nothing." Without staying connected to Jesus through prayer, we cannot bear fruit or fulfill God's purposes for our lives. By making prayer a priority, we acknowledge our need for God and stay connected to the source of our strength and wisdom.

Prayer is also a powerful tool for resisting temptation and spiritual attacks. In Matthew 26:41, Jesus advised His disciples, "Watch and pray, that ye enter not into temptation: the spirit indeed is willing, but the flesh is weak." Prayer strengthens our spirit and helps us to resist the temptations that can lead us away from God. By staying vigilant in prayer, we can guard our hearts and minds against the enemy's schemes and remain faithful to God's commandments.

Teaching the next generation about the importance of prayer is crucial. Proverbs 22:6 advises, "Train up a child in the way he should go: and when he is old, he will not depart from it." By modeling and teaching prayer to children and young people, we help them develop a strong foundation of faith and dependence on God. This includes encouraging them to pray regularly, teaching them how to pray, and involving them in family and corporate prayer. By instilling these values early on, we prepare them to live lives of prayer and reliance on God.

The church community plays a significant role in promoting prayer among its members. Hebrews 10:24-25 says, "And let us consider one another to provoke unto love and to good works: Not forsaking the assembling of ourselves together, as the manner of some is; but exhorting one another: and so much the more, as ye see the day approaching." By encouraging and supporting one another in prayer, Christians can help each other stay committed to a vibrant prayer life. The church can provide teaching, resources, and opportunities for prayer, fostering a culture of dependence on God.

Prayer also involves thanksgiving and praise. Philippians 4:6-7 reminds us to include thanksgiving in our prayers: "Be careful for nothing; but in every thing by prayer and supplication with thanksgiving let your requests be made known unto God. And the peace of God, which passeth all understanding, shall keep your hearts and minds through Christ Jesus." By thanking God for His blessings and praising Him for His goodness, we cultivate a heart of gratitude and recognize His work in our lives. This attitude of thanksgiving enhances our prayer life and deepens our relationship with God.

In addition to regular prayer, fasting can be a powerful complement to prayer. Matthew 6:17-18 says, "But thou, when thou fastest, anoint thine head, and wash thy face; That thou appear not unto men to fast, but unto thy Father which is in secret: and thy Father, which seeth in secret, shall reward thee openly." Fasting, combined with prayer, helps us to focus more intently on God, seek His will, and experience spiritual breakthroughs. By setting aside time to fast and pray, we demonstrate our hunger for God and our commitment to seeking His guidance and intervention.

In conclusion, prayer is a fundamental principle in the Christian faith, emphasizing constant communication with God and reliance on His guidance and strength. 1 Thessalonians 5:17 teaches us to "pray without ceasing," highlighting the importance of maintaining a continuous and consistent prayer life. Despite the neglect of prayer and reliance on self in today's world, Christians are called to cultivate a strong prayer life. This involves acknowledging our dependence on God, seeking His will, interceding for others, and participating in both personal and corporate prayer. By making prayer a priority, teaching the next generation, and supporting one another within the church community, we can live lives of prayer and reliance on God. This commitment to prayer not only strengthens our relationship with God but also empowers us to fulfill His purposes and resist temptation. Through prayer, we experience God's peace, guidance, and strength, making a lasting impact on our lives and the lives of those around us. By embracing the call to pray without ceasing, we can walk closely with the Lord and reflect His love and grace to the world.

Chapter 20 - Scripture Study

Scripture study is a fundamental aspect of the Christian faith, emphasizing the importance of knowing and understanding God's Word to guide our lives. 2 Timothy 3:16-17 says, "All scripture is given by inspiration of God, and is profitable for doctrine, for reproof, for correction, for instruction in righteousness: That the man of God may be perfect, throughly furnished unto all good works." This verse highlights that the Bible is God-inspired and essential for teaching, rebuking, correcting, and training in righteousness. In today's world, ignorance of and indifference to Biblical teaching are prevalent, leading people away from the truths that Scripture provides. As Christians, it is crucial to commit to studying the Bible, applying its teachings to our lives, and allowing it to shape our walk with the Lord.

Studying Scripture begins with recognizing its divine inspiration and authority. The Bible is not just a collection of historical documents or moral teachings; it is the inspired Word of God. 2 Peter 1:20-21 states, "Knowing this first, that no prophecy of the scripture is of any private interpretation. For the prophecy came not in old time by the will of man: but holy men of God spake as they were moved by the Holy Ghost." This passage teaches that the Scriptures were written by men who were inspired by the Holy Spirit, making the Bible a trustworthy and authoritative guide for our lives. By acknowledging the Bible's divine origin, we approach it with the reverence and respect it deserves.

One of the primary purposes of Scripture study is to learn sound doctrine. Doctrine refers to the set of beliefs that Christians hold based on the teachings of the Bible. Romans 15:4 says, "For whatsoever things were written aforetime were written for our learning, that we through patience and comfort of the scriptures might have hope." By studying the Bible, we learn about God's nature, His plan for salvation, and His expectations for our lives. This understanding helps us develop a strong foundation of faith, guiding our beliefs and actions in accordance with God's truth.

Scripture study is also essential for reproof and correction. The Bible exposes our sins and shortcomings, convicting us of the areas in our lives that need to change. Hebrews 4:12 says, "For the word of God is quick, and powerful, and sharper than any twoedged sword, piercing even to the dividing asunder of soul and spirit, and of the joints and marrow, and is a discerner of the thoughts and intents of the heart." God's Word penetrates our hearts, revealing our true thoughts and intentions. By studying Scripture, we allow God to correct us and transform our lives, aligning our actions and attitudes with His will.

In addition to teaching and correcting, Scripture provides instruction in righteousness. Psalm 119:105 says, "Thy word is a lamp unto my feet, and a light unto my path." The Bible guides us in making wise decisions and living a life that honors God. It offers practical advice on how to handle various situations, relationships, and challenges we face. By following the principles found in Scripture, we can navigate life with confidence and integrity, knowing that we are walking in God's ways.

Despite the importance of Scripture study, many people today are ignorant of and indifferent to Biblical teaching. Hosea 4:6 warns, "My people are destroyed for lack of knowledge: because thou hast rejected knowledge, I will also reject thee." Ignorance of God's Word leads to spiritual destruction, as people are unable to discern truth from falsehood or live according to God's standards. Indifference to the Bible results in a lack of spiritual growth and a weakened faith. As Christians, we must prioritize Scripture study to avoid these pitfalls and strengthen our relationship with God.

One way to deepen our Scripture study is through regular reading and meditation on the Bible. Joshua 1:8 advises, "This book of the law shall not depart out of thy mouth; but thou shalt meditate therein day and night, that thou mayest observe to do according to all that is written therein: for then thou shalt make thy way prosperous, and then thou shalt have good success." By consistently reading and reflecting on God's Word, we internalize its teachings and allow it to shape our thoughts and actions. This daily practice helps us stay connected to God and grow in our understanding of His will.

Prayer is also a vital component of effective Scripture study. Psalm 119:18 says, "Open thou mine eyes, that I may behold wondrous things out of thy law." By praying for understanding and wisdom, we invite the Holy Spirit to illuminate the Scriptures and reveal their deeper meanings to us. James 1:5 encourages, "If any of you lack wisdom, let him ask of God, that giveth to all men liberally, and upbraideth not; and it shall be given him." Seeking God's guidance in prayer enhances our study of the Bible and helps us apply its teachings to our lives.

Another important aspect of Scripture study is discussing and sharing insights with others. Acts 17:11 describes the Bereans, who were commended for their eagerness to learn and verify the truth of the Scriptures: "These were more noble than those in Thessalonica, in that they received the word with all readiness of mind, and searched the scriptures daily, whether those things were so." By studying the Bible with others, we gain different perspectives and deepen our understanding. This practice also fosters accountability and encouragement, helping us stay committed to our study and application of God's Word.

Memorizing Scripture is another valuable discipline that enhances our study and application of the Bible. Psalm 119:11 says, "Thy word have I hid in mine heart, that I might not sin against thee." By committing verses to memory, we can recall God's promises and instructions in times of need. This helps us resist temptation, make wise decisions, and stay focused on God's truth. Memorization also allows us to meditate on God's Word throughout the day, keeping our minds and hearts aligned with His will.

Scripture study is not only about gaining knowledge but also about transformation. Romans 12:2 teaches, "And be not conformed to this world: but be ye transformed by the renewing of your mind, that ye may prove what is that good, and acceptable, and perfect, will of God." As we study the Bible, our minds are renewed, and our lives are transformed to reflect Christ's character. This transformation impacts every area of our lives, including our relationships, decisions, and actions. By allowing God's Word to change us, we become more like Jesus and better equipped to serve Him.

Teaching the next generation about the importance of Scripture study is also crucial. Deuteronomy 6:6-7 instructs, "And these words, which I command thee this day, shall be in thine heart: And thou shalt teach them diligently unto thy children, and shalt talk of them when thou sittest in thine house, and when thou walkest by the way, and when thou liest down, and when thou risest up." By modeling and teaching Scripture study to children and young people, we help them develop a strong foundation of faith and a love for God's Word. This includes reading the Bible together, discussing its teachings, and encouraging them to memorize verses. By instilling these habits early on, we prepare them to live lives grounded in God's truth.

The church community plays a significant role in promoting Scripture study among its members. Hebrews 10:24-25 says, "And let us consider one another to provoke unto love and to good works: Not forsaking the assembling of ourselves together, as the manner of some is; but exhorting one another: and so much the more, as ye see the day approaching." By encouraging and supporting one another in studying the Bible, Christians can help each other grow in their understanding and application of God's Word. The church can provide teaching, resources, and opportunities for group study, fostering a culture of learning and spiritual growth.

Despite the many benefits of Scripture study, there are attacks on its importance and relevance in today's world. Many people view the

Bible as outdated or irrelevant, neglecting its teachings and relying on their own understanding. Proverbs 3:7 warns, "Be not wise in thine own eyes: fear the Lord, and depart from evil." By ignoring God's Word, people miss out on the wisdom and guidance it offers, leading to spiritual confusion and moral decay. As Christians, we must counter these attacks by demonstrating the value and relevance of Scripture in our lives and encouraging others to do the same.

In conclusion, Scripture study is a fundamental aspect of the Christian faith, emphasizing the importance of knowing and understanding God's Word to guide our lives. 2 Timothy 3:16-17 teaches that all Scripture is inspired by God and is essential for teaching, rebuking, correcting, and training in righteousness. Despite the prevalence of ignorance and indifference to Biblical teaching in today's world, Christians are called to commit to studying the Bible and applying its teachings to their lives. This involves regular reading and meditation, prayer, discussion with others, memorization, and allowing the Bible to transform our minds and hearts. By making Scripture study a priority, teaching the next generation, and supporting one another within the church community, we can live lives grounded in God's truth. This commitment to Scripture study not only strengthens our relationship with God but also equips us to fulfill His purposes and resist the attacks on its importance and relevance. Through the diligent study of God's Word, we experience His guidance, wisdom, and strength, making a lasting impact on our lives and the lives of those around us. By embracing the call to study Scripture, we can walk closely with the Lord and reflect His love and grace to the world.

Chapter 21 - Contentment

Contentment is a fundamental principle in the Christian faith, emphasizing the importance of being satisfied with what we have and trusting in God's provision. Philippians 4:11 says, "Not that I speak in respect of want: for I have learned, in whatsoever state I am, therewith to be content." This verse highlights the value of contentment, teaching us that it is a state of mind we can learn, regardless of our circumstances. In today's world, consumerism and discontent are prevalent, driving people to constantly seek more and never feel satisfied. As Christians, it is essential to cultivate a heart of contentment, reflecting our trust in the Lord and His sufficiency in our lives.

Contentment begins with understanding that everything we have comes from God and trusting in His provision. James 1:17 reminds us, "Every good gift and every perfect gift is from above, and cometh down from the Father of lights, with whom is no variableness, neither shadow of turning." Recognizing that all our blessings come from God helps us to be grateful and content with what we have. By trusting in God's provision, we can find peace and satisfaction, knowing that He will meet our needs according to His perfect plan.

One aspect of contentment is gratitude. 1 Thessalonians 5:18 instructs, "In every thing give thanks: for this is the will of God in Christ Jesus concerning you." Being thankful for what we have, rather than focusing on what we lack, fosters a sense of contentment. Gratitude shifts our perspective from one of scarcity to one of abundance, helping us to see the blessings in our lives. By developing a habit of thankfulness, we can cultivate a contented heart that recognizes and appreciates God's goodness.

Contentment also involves trusting in God's timing and plan for our lives. Proverbs 3:5-6 says, "Trust in the Lord with all thine heart; and lean not unto thine own understanding. In all thy ways acknowledge him, and he shall direct thy paths." Trusting in God's plan means believing that He knows what is best for us and that His timing is perfect. When we rely on our understanding and try to control our circumstances, we often become anxious and discontented. By surrendering our plans to God and trusting in His wisdom, we can find peace and contentment in every situation.

Another important aspect of contentment is learning to be satisfied with what we have, rather than constantly seeking more. Hebrews 13:5 advises, "Let your conversation be without covetousness; and be content with such things as ye have: for he hath said, I will never leave thee, nor forsake thee." Covetousness, or the desire for more, leads to discontent and a constant sense of lack. By focusing on God's promise to always be with us and provide for us, we can find contentment in our current circumstances.

The apostle Paul provides a powerful example of contentment in Philippians 4:12-13, where he writes, "I know both how to be abased, and I know how to abound: every where and in all things I am instructed both to be full and to be hungry, both to abound and to suffer need. I can do all things through Christ which strengtheneth me." Paul learned to be content in every situation, whether he had plenty or was in need, because he relied on Christ's strength. This teaches us that true contentment comes from our relationship with Christ and not from our external circumstances.

Prayer is a vital component of developing contentment. By bringing our needs and desires before God in prayer, we can find peace and trust in His provision. Philippians 4:6-7 encourages, "Be careful for nothing; but in every thing by prayer and supplication with thanksgiving let your requests be made known unto God. And the peace of God, which passeth all understanding, shall keep your hearts and minds through Christ Jesus." Through prayer, we can release our worries and anxieties to God, allowing His peace to fill our hearts and minds. This peace enables us to be content, knowing that God is in control and will take care of us.

Teaching the next generation about contentment is also crucial. Proverbs 22:6 advises, "Train up a child in the way he should go: and when he is old, he will not depart from it." By modeling and teaching contentment to children and young people, we help them develop strong moral values and a commitment to gratitude and trust in God. This includes teaching them the importance of being thankful for what they have, avoiding the constant pursuit of more, and trusting in God's provision. By instilling these values early on, we prepare them to live contented lives that honor God.

The church community plays a significant role in promoting contentment among its members. Hebrews 10:24-25 says, "And let us consider one another to provoke unto love and to good works: Not forsaking the assembling of ourselves together, as the manner of some is; but exhorting one another: and so much the more, as ye see the day approaching." By encouraging and supporting one another, Christians can help each other stay committed to living contentedly. The church can provide teaching, resources, and opportunities for service, fostering a culture of gratitude and trust in God's provision.

Contentment also involves avoiding the traps of consumerism and materialism. Jesus warns in Luke 12:15, "And he said unto them, Take heed, and beware of covetousness: for a man's life consisteth not in the abundance of the things which he possesseth." Our worth and fulfillment do not come from material possessions but from our relationship with God. By focusing on spiritual growth and eternal treasures, rather than earthly wealth, we can find true contentment. Matthew 6:19-21 advises, "Lay not up for yourselves treasures upon earth, where moth and rust doth corrupt, and where thieves break through and steal: But lay up for yourselves treasures in heaven, where neither moth nor rust doth corrupt, and where thieves do not break through nor steal: For where your treasure is, there will your heart be also." By prioritizing spiritual over material wealth, we can cultivate a heart of contentment.

Contentment also means being willing to share what we have with others. 1 Timothy 6:17-19 instructs, "Charge them that are rich in this world, that they be not highminded, nor trust in uncertain riches, but in the living God, who giveth us richly all things to enjoy; That they do good, that they be rich in good works, ready to distribute, willing to communicate; Laying up in store for themselves a good foundation against the time to come, that they may lay hold on eternal life." By being generous and willing to share our resources, we demonstrate our trust in God's provision and our contentment with what we have. This generosity not only blesses others but also strengthens our own sense of fulfillment and joy.

Despite the many benefits of contentment, consumerism and discontent are significant challenges in today's world. Advertisements, social media, and societal pressures constantly encourage us to seek more and compare ourselves to others, leading to feelings of inadequacy and dissatisfaction. As Christians, we must counter these influences by focusing on God's truth and cultivating a heart of contentment. Romans 12:2 teaches, "And be not conformed to this world: but be ye transformed by the renewing of your mind, that ye may prove what is that good, and acceptable, and perfect, will of God." By renewing our minds with God's Word and aligning our desires with His will, we can resist the pull of consumerism and find true contentment.

Contentment is also about finding joy in the present moment and appreciating the simple blessings of life. Ecclesiastes 3:12-13 says, "I know that there is no good in them, but for a man to rejoice, and to do good in his life. And also that every man should eat and drink, and enjoy the good of all his labour, it is the gift of God." By focusing on the present and being grateful for the small joys and blessings, we can cultivate a heart of contentment. This means taking time to appreciate our relationships, the beauty of creation, and the simple pleasures of daily life.

In conclusion, contentment is a fundamental principle in the Christian faith, emphasizing the importance of being satisfied with what we have and trusting in God's provision. Philippians 4:11 teaches us to be content in all circumstances, recognizing that contentment is a state of mind we can learn. Despite the prevalence of consumerism and discontent in today's world, Christians are called to cultivate a heart of contentment. This involves understanding that everything we have comes from God, practicing gratitude, trusting in God's timing and plan, and avoiding the constant pursuit of more. By making contentment a priority, teaching the next generation, and supporting one another within the church community, we can live lives grounded in gratitude and trust in God's provision. This commitment to contentment not only strengthens our relationship with God but also brings peace and fulfillment to our lives. Through contentment, we demonstrate our trust in God's sufficiency and reflect His love and grace to the world. By embracing the call to be content, we can walk closely with the Lord and experience the true joy and satisfaction that comes from a life rooted in His provision and care.

Chapter 22 - Respect for Authority

Respect for authority is a crucial principle in the Christian faith, emphasizing the importance of honoring and obeying those in positions of power, as they are instituted by God. Romans 13:1 says, "Let every soul be subject unto the higher powers. For there is no power but of God: the powers that be are ordained of God." This verse teaches that all authority comes from God, and respecting authority is an act of obedience to Him. In today's world, there is a widespread disregard for authority and a spirit of rebellion, which undermines social order and spiritual growth. As Christians, it is essential to cultivate a respectful attitude towards authority, reflecting our submission to God and His ordained structures.

Understanding that all authority is established by God is the foundation of respect for authority. Proverbs 8:15-16 says, "By me kings reign, and princes decree justice. By me princes rule, and nobles, even all the judges of the earth." This passage shows that God is the ultimate source of all authority and governance. Recognizing this helps us to see that respecting authority is, in fact, respecting God's divine order. When we honor those in authority, we acknowledge God's sovereignty and His control over the affairs of men.

One aspect of respect for authority is obedience to laws and regulations. Titus 3:1 instructs, "Put them in mind to be subject to principalities and powers, to obey magistrates, to be ready to every good work." Obeying laws and following rules is a practical way to show respect for authority. This includes obeying traffic laws, paying taxes, and following workplace regulations. By doing so, we contribute to a peaceful and orderly society, which is pleasing to God. Romans 13:7 further emphasizes this: "Render therefore to all their dues: tribute to whom tribute is due; custom to whom custom; fear to whom fear;

honour to whom honour." By fulfilling our civic duties, we demonstrate our respect for the authorities God has placed over us.

Respect for authority also involves honoring those in leadership positions, even when we disagree with them. 1 Peter 2:17 says, "Honour all men. Love the brotherhood. Fear God. Honour the king." This verse calls us to honor and respect all people, including those in authority, regardless of their actions or policies. It is possible to disagree respectfully, maintaining a posture of honor and humility. This attitude reflects our trust in God's ultimate control and our commitment to His commands.

In the family, respect for authority starts with children honoring their parents. Ephesians 6:1-3 says, "Children, obey your parents in the Lord: for this is right. Honour thy father and mother; which is the first commandment with promise; That it may be well with thee, and thou mayest live long on the earth." Teaching children to respect their parents lays the foundation for respecting other authorities in their lives. This respect fosters a sense of order and discipline, which is essential for their development and well-being. Parents, in turn, are called to guide their children with love and fairness, as stated in Ephesians 6:4: "And, ye fathers, provoke not your children to wrath: but bring them up in the nurture and admonition of the Lord."

In the workplace, respect for authority means honoring our employers and supervisors. Colossians 3:22-24 instructs, "Servants, obey in all things your masters according to the flesh; not with eyeservice, as menpleasers; but in singleness of heart, fearing God: And whatsoever ye do, do it heartily, as to the Lord, and not unto men; Knowing that of the Lord ye shall receive the reward of the inheritance: for ye serve the Lord Christ." By working diligently and respectfully, we reflect our commitment to God's standards and our recognition of His authority over all aspects of our lives. This attitude not only honors God but also sets a positive example for others in the workplace.

In the church, respect for authority means honoring church leaders and submitting to their guidance. Hebrews 13:17 says, "Obey them that have the rule over you, and submit yourselves: for they watch for your souls, as they that must give account, that they may do it with joy, and not with grief: for that is unprofitable for you." Church leaders are responsible for guiding and nurturing the spiritual well-being of the congregation. By respecting their authority, we support their ministry and contribute to the unity and growth of the church. This respect includes being open to their teaching, following their leadership, and supporting them in prayer.

Despite the importance of respecting authority, there are times when authorities may act unjustly or contrary to God's commands. In such cases, we are called to obey God rather than men. Acts 5:29 says, "Then Peter and the other apostles answered and said, We ought to obey God rather than men." When authorities require us to act against God's Word, we must respectfully and courageously stand for our faith. This may involve peaceful resistance, speaking out against injustice, or enduring persecution for righteousness' sake. By maintaining our commitment to God's principles, we honor His authority above all others.

Prayer is a vital component of respecting authority. 1 Timothy 2:1-2 encourages, "I exhort therefore, that, first of all, supplications, prayers, intercessions, and giving of thanks, be made for all men; For kings, and for all that are in authority; that we may lead a quiet and peaceable life in all godliness and honesty." Praying for those in authority helps us to develop a heart of respect and compassion for them. It also invites God's wisdom and guidance for leaders, contributing to the well-being of society. By committing to pray for our leaders, we demonstrate our trust in God's sovereignty and our desire to see His will accomplished through them.

Teaching the next generation about respect for authority is also crucial. Proverbs 22:6 advises, "Train up a child in the way he should go: and when he is old, he will not depart from it." By modeling and teaching respect for authority to children and young people, we help them develop strong moral values and a commitment to order and discipline. This includes teaching them to honor their parents, obey teachers and school rules, and respect laws and government officials. By instilling these values early on, we prepare them to live lives that honor God and contribute positively to society.

The church community plays a significant role in promoting respect for authority among its members. Hebrews 10:24-25 says, "And let us consider one another to provoke unto love and to good works: Not forsaking the assembling of ourselves together, as the manner of some is; but exhorting one another: and so much the more, as ye see the day approaching." By encouraging and supporting one another, Christians can help each other stay committed to respecting authority. The church can provide teaching, resources, and opportunities for service, fostering a culture of honor and submission to God's ordained structures.

Despite the many benefits of respecting authority, rebellion and disregard for authority are significant challenges in today's world. Society often promotes individualism and self-reliance, leading to a lack of respect for those in positions of power. This attitude undermines social order and spiritual growth, as it fosters a spirit of pride and disobedience. As Christians, we must counter these influences by focusing on God's truth and cultivating a heart of respect for authority. Romans 12:2 teaches, "And be not conformed to this world: but be ye transformed by the renewing of your mind, that ye may prove what is that good, and acceptable, and perfect, will of God." By renewing our minds with God's Word and aligning our attitudes with His will, we can resist the pull of rebellion and live lives that honor Him.

Respect for authority also involves recognizing the limits of our own understanding and submitting to God's wisdom. Proverbs 3:7

warns, "Be not wise in thine own eyes: fear the Lord, and depart from evil." Humility and a willingness to submit to God's guidance help us to respect those He has placed in authority over us. This attitude fosters a sense of dependence on God and a commitment to His principles, leading to a life of obedience and honor.

In conclusion, respect for authority is a crucial principle in the Christian faith, emphasizing the importance of honoring and obeying those in positions of power, as they are instituted by God. Romans 13:1 teaches us that all authority comes from God, and respecting authority is an act of obedience to Him. Despite the prevalence of rebellion and disregard for authority in today's world, Christians are called to cultivate a respectful attitude towards authority. This involves understanding that all authority is established by God, obeying laws and regulations, honoring leaders even when we disagree, and maintaining a posture of humility and submission. By making respect for authority a priority, teaching the next generation, and supporting one another within the church community, we can live lives grounded in obedience and honor to God's ordained structures. This commitment to respect for authority not only strengthens our relationship with God but also contributes to social order and spiritual growth. Through respect for authority, we demonstrate our trust in God's sovereignty and reflect His love and grace to the world. By embracing the call to respect authority, we can walk closely with the Lord and experience the true peace and order that come from a life rooted in His provision and care.

Chapter 23 - Gratitude

Gratitude is a vital principle in the Christian faith, emphasizing the importance of being thankful in all circumstances and recognizing God's blessings in our lives. 1 Thessalonians 5:18 says, "In every thing give thanks: for this is the will of God in Christ Jesus concerning you." This verse teaches that gratitude is not just a suggestion but a command from God. It is His will that we cultivate a thankful heart. In today's world, ingratitude and entitlement are widespread, leading people away from a heart of thankfulness and towards a life of dissatisfaction and selfishness. As Christians, it is essential to develop an attitude of gratitude, reflecting our trust in God's goodness and recognizing His hand in every aspect of our lives.

Gratitude begins with recognizing that everything we have comes from God. James 1:17 reminds us, "Every good gift and every perfect gift is from above, and cometh down from the Father of lights, with whom is no variableness, neither shadow of turning." By acknowledging that all our blessings come from God, we develop a heart of thankfulness. This understanding helps us to appreciate even the smallest blessings and to see God's hand at work in our lives. When we recognize God's provision, we are more likely to be content and satisfied, knowing that He is taking care of us.

One aspect of gratitude is expressing thanks in all circumstances, not just when things are going well. Philippians 4:6-7 encourages, "Be careful for nothing; but in every thing by prayer and supplication with thanksgiving let your requests be made known unto God. And the peace of God, which passeth all understanding, shall keep your hearts and minds through Christ Jesus." By presenting our requests to God with thanksgiving, we acknowledge His sovereignty and trust in His plan for our lives. This attitude of gratitude brings peace to our hearts and minds, even in challenging situations, because we know that God is in control and working for our good.

Gratitude also involves remembering and recounting God's past faithfulness. Psalm 103:2 says, "Bless the Lord, O my soul, and forget not all his benefits." By reflecting on God's past blessings and faithfulness, we reinforce our trust in Him and cultivate a spirit of thankfulness. This practice helps us to stay focused on God's goodness, especially during difficult times, and to maintain a hopeful and positive outlook. By regularly remembering and giving thanks for God's past works, we build a foundation of gratitude that sustains us through life's ups and downs.

Ingratitude and entitlement are significant barriers to developing a thankful heart. Romans 1:21 warns, "Because that, when they knew God, they glorified him not as God, neither were thankful; but became vain in their imaginations, and their foolish heart was darkened." Ingratitude leads to a hardened heart and a lack of recognition for God's blessings. Entitlement, on the other hand, fosters a mindset that we deserve more than we have, leading to dissatisfaction and resentment. As Christians, we must combat these attitudes by actively practicing gratitude and humility, recognizing that we are dependent on God's grace and mercy for everything we have.

Gratitude is also expressed through our actions and attitudes towards others. Colossians 3:15 says, "And let the peace of God rule in your hearts, to the which also ye are called in one body; and be ye thankful." By living out our gratitude, we demonstrate God's love and grace to those around us. This includes being kind, generous, and forgiving, as these actions reflect a thankful heart. When we are grateful, we are more likely to share our blessings with others and to build positive, supportive relationships that honor God.

Prayer is a crucial component of developing gratitude. By regularly communicating with God and expressing our thanks, we cultivate a habit of thankfulness. Philippians 4:6-7, mentioned earlier, highlights the importance of thanksgiving in prayer. By bringing our requests to God with a thankful heart, we not only acknowledge His provision but also reinforce our trust in His plan. This practice helps us to stay connected to God and to maintain a positive and grateful outlook, even in challenging times.

Teaching the next generation about gratitude is also essential. Proverbs 22:6 advises, "Train up a child in the way he should go: and when he is old, he will not depart from it." By modeling and teaching gratitude to children and young people, we help them develop strong moral values and a commitment to thankfulness. This includes encouraging them to say thank you, to appreciate what they have, and to recognize God's blessings in their lives. By instilling these values early on, we prepare them to live lives of gratitude that honor God.

The church community plays a significant role in promoting gratitude among its members. Hebrews 10:24-25 says, "And let us consider one another to provoke unto love and to good works: Not forsaking the assembling of ourselves together, as the manner of some is; but exhorting one another: and so much the more, as ye see the day approaching." By encouraging and supporting one another, Christians can help each other stay committed to a thankful attitude. The church can provide teaching, resources, and opportunities for service, fostering a culture of gratitude and appreciation for God's blessings.

Despite the many benefits of gratitude, ingratitude and entitlement are significant challenges in today's world. Society often promotes a sense of entitlement, leading people to believe they deserve more than they have and to be dissatisfied with their circumstances. This attitude undermines the development of a thankful heart and leads to a lack of appreciation for God's blessings. As Christians, we must counter these influences by focusing on God's truth and cultivating a heart of gratitude. Romans 12:2 teaches, "And be not conformed to this world: but be ye transformed by the renewing of your mind, that ye may prove what is that good, and acceptable, and perfect, will of God." By renewing our minds with God's Word and aligning our attitudes with His will, we can resist the pull of ingratitude and live lives that honor Him.

Gratitude also involves recognizing and appreciating the simple blessings in life. Ecclesiastes 3:12-13 says, "I know that there is no good in them, but for a man to rejoice, and to do good in his life. And also that every man should eat and drink, and enjoy the good of all his labour, it is the gift of God." By focusing on the present and being grateful for the small joys and blessings, we can cultivate a heart of thankfulness. This means taking time to appreciate our relationships, the beauty of creation, and the simple pleasures of daily life.

In conclusion, gratitude is a vital principle in the Christian faith, emphasizing the importance of being thankful in all circumstances and recognizing God's blessings in our lives. 1 Thessalonians 5:18 teaches us to give thanks in everything, highlighting that gratitude is God's will for us. Despite the prevalence of ingratitude and entitlement in today's world, Christians are called to develop an attitude of gratitude. This involves recognizing that everything we have comes from God, expressing thanks in all circumstances, remembering God's past faithfulness, and living out our gratitude through our actions and attitudes. By making gratitude a priority, teaching the next generation, and supporting one another within the church community, we can live lives grounded in thankfulness and trust in God's provision. This commitment to gratitude not only strengthens our relationship with God but also brings peace and fulfillment to our lives. Through gratitude, we demonstrate our trust in God's goodness and reflect His love and grace to the world. By embracing the call to be thankful, we can walk closely with the Lord and experience the true joy and satisfaction that come from a life rooted in His blessings and care.

Chapter 24 - Unity in Christ

Unity in Christ is a fundamental principle in the Christian faith, emphasizing the importance of being united as one body despite our differences. Galatians 3:28 says, "There is neither Jew nor Greek, there is neither bond nor free, there is neither male nor female: for ye are all one in Christ Jesus." This verse teaches that in Christ, all barriers are broken down, and we are united as one. In today's world, division and prejudice are rampant, causing strife and disunity among people. As Christians, it is essential to cultivate and maintain unity in Christ, reflecting His love and breaking down barriers that divide us.

Understanding that we are all one in Christ begins with recognizing that Jesus' sacrifice was for everyone, regardless of background or status. John 3:16 says, "For God so loved the world, that he gave his only begotten Son, that whosoever believeth in him should not perish, but have everlasting life." Jesus' love and sacrifice were for the whole world, not just a select group of people. By accepting this truth, we can appreciate the diversity within the body of Christ and work towards unity.

One aspect of unity is embracing our differences and seeing them as strengths rather than sources of division. 1 Corinthians 12:12-14 says, "For as the body is one, and hath many members, and all the members of that one body, being many, are one body: so also is Christ. For by one Spirit are we all baptized into one body, whether we be Jews or Gentiles, whether we be bond or free; and have been all made to drink into one Spirit. For the body is not one member, but many." This passage teaches that just as the human body has many different parts that work together, the body of Christ is made up of diverse members who each play a vital role. By appreciating and valuing each other's unique contributions, we can foster unity and work together more effectively.

Unity also involves breaking down prejudices and stereotypes that cause division. James 2:1 says, "My brethren, have not the faith of our Lord Jesus Christ, the Lord of glory, with respect of persons." This verse reminds us that showing favoritism or prejudice is inconsistent with our faith in Christ. Instead, we are called to love and accept one another as Christ loves and accepts us. By challenging our own prejudices and working to overcome them, we can build a more inclusive and united community.

Prayer is a crucial component of fostering unity. Jesus prayed for the unity of all believers in John 17:20-23: "Neither pray I for these alone, but for them also which shall believe on me through their word; That they all may be one; as thou, Father, art in me, and I in thee, that they also may be one in us: that the world may believe that thou hast sent me. And the glory which thou gavest me I have given them; that they may be one, even as we are one: I in them, and thou in me, that they may be made perfect in one; and that the world may know that thou hast sent me, and hast loved them, as thou hast loved me." By praying for unity and asking God to help us overcome divisions, we align ourselves with Jesus' desire for His followers to be united.

In the church, unity is essential for effective ministry and witness. Ephesians 4:3-6 says, "Endeavouring to keep the unity of the Spirit in the bond of peace. There is one body, and one Spirit, even as ye are called in one hope of your calling; One Lord, one faith, one baptism, One God and Father of all, who is above all, and through all, and in you all." This passage emphasizes the importance of maintaining unity through the Spirit and recognizing our shared faith and mission. By working together in harmony, the church can more effectively spread the gospel and demonstrate the love of Christ to the world.

Despite the importance of unity, division and prejudice are significant challenges in today's world. Society often promotes individualism and competition, leading to strife and division. As Christians, we must counter these influences by focusing on God's truth and cultivating a spirit of unity. Romans 12:16 says, "Be of the same mind one toward another. Mind not high things, but condescend to men of low estate. Be not wise in your own conceits." By humbling ourselves and valuing others, we can build unity and harmony within the body of Christ.

Forgiveness is also vital for maintaining unity. Colossians 3:12-14 says, "Put on therefore, as the elect of God, holy and beloved, bowels of mercies, kindness, humbleness of mind, meekness, longsuffering; Forbearing one another, and forgiving one another, if any man have a quarrel against any: even as Christ forgave you, so also do ye. And above all these things put on charity, which is the bond of perfectness." By forgiving one another and showing love, we can overcome conflicts and build stronger relationships. Forgiveness breaks down barriers and fosters reconciliation, essential for unity.

Teaching the next generation about the importance of unity is also crucial. Proverbs 22:6 advises, "Train up a child in the way he should go: and when he is old, he will not depart from it." By modeling and teaching unity to children and young people, we help them develop strong moral values and a commitment to harmony. This includes encouraging them to appreciate diversity, challenge prejudices, and work together with others. By instilling these values early on, we prepare them to live lives that honor God and promote unity.

The church community plays a significant role in promoting unity among its members. Hebrews 10:24-25 says, "And let us consider one another to provoke unto love and to good works: Not forsaking the assembling of ourselves together, as the manner of some is; but exhorting one another: and so much the more, as ye see the day approaching." By encouraging and supporting one another, Christians can help each other stay committed to unity. The church can provide teaching, resources, and opportunities for fellowship and service, fostering a culture of unity and cooperation.

Despite the many benefits of unity, division and prejudice are significant challenges in today's world. Society often promotes individualism and competition, leading to strife and division. As Christians, we must counter these influences by focusing on God's truth and cultivating a spirit of unity. Romans 12:16 teaches, "Be of the same mind one toward another. Mind not high things, but condescend to men of low estate. Be not wise in your own conceits." By humbling ourselves and valuing others, we can build unity and harmony within the body of Christ.

Unity also involves working together towards common goals and supporting one another in our spiritual journeys. Ecclesiastes 4:9-12 says, "Two are better than one; because they have a good reward for their labour. For if they fall, the one will lift up his fellow: but woe to him that is alone when he falleth; for he hath not another to help him up. Again, if two lie together, then they have heat: but how can one be warm alone? And if one prevail against him, two shall withstand him; and a threefold cord is not quickly broken." By supporting and encouraging each other, we strengthen our unity and can accomplish more together than we could alone.

In conclusion, unity in Christ is a fundamental principle in the Christian faith, emphasizing the importance of being united as one body despite our differences. Galatians 3:28 teaches us that in Christ, all barriers are broken down, and we are united as one. Despite the prevalence of division and prejudice in today's world, Christians are called to cultivate and maintain unity in Christ. This involves embracing our differences, breaking down prejudices, praying for unity, and working together in harmony. By making unity a priority, teaching the next generation, and supporting one another within the church community, we can live lives grounded in the love and unity of Christ. This commitment to unity not only strengthens our relationship with God but also enhances our witness to the world. Through unity, we demonstrate the love and grace of God, making a lasting impact on those around us. By embracing the call to be united in Christ, we can walk closely with the Lord and experience the true joy and strength that come from a life rooted in His love and unity.

Conclusion

As we reach the conclusion of "Under Fire: The Sanctity of the Traditional Biblical Home," it's clear that the traditional family, as taught in the Bible, is under serious pressure in today's world. Throughout this book, we've explored how the biblical model for the family is being challenged and why it's so important to defend it. The traditional biblical home isn't just an old idea; it's a strong foundation that God designed to bring love, stability, and faith into our lives.

The roles of husbands, wives, and children, as outlined in Scripture, are not just suggestions—they are part of God's perfect plan for how families should function. When we follow these roles, our homes can become places of peace, support, and spiritual growth. But when we stray from these principles, we risk causing confusion and hurt within our families.

Now, the question is: What can you do to protect the traditional biblical home? The first step is to make God the center of your home. This means reading the Bible regularly, praying together as a family, and discussing what you learn from God's Word. By doing this, you'll build a strong foundation that can withstand the challenges of the world.

Next, take your role in the family seriously. Whether you're a parent, spouse, or child, you have an important part to play in making your home a place of love and respect. Support each other, work as a team, and always strive to follow God's guidance.

Finally, don't be afraid to stand up for the biblical family values. In a world that often opposes these values, your commitment can make a big difference. By living out these principles, you help ensure that the sanctity of the traditional biblical home remains strong for future generations.

Don't miss out!

Visit the website below and you can sign up to receive emails whenever Joshua Rhoades publishes a new book. There's no charge and no obligation.

https://books2read.com/r/B-A-AJLBB-UNPUE

BOOKS 2 READ

Connecting independent readers to independent writers.

Did you love *Under Fire- The Sanctity of the Traditional Biblical Home*? Then you should read *Flee Fornication: The Plea For Purity*[1] by Joshua Rhoades!

[2]

"Flee Fornication - The Plea For Purity" is an essential read for anyone grappling with the challenges of maintaining sexual purity in a world that often glorifies the opposite. This book dives deep into the spiritual and moral pitfalls that can ensnare individuals, drawing them away from a life of purity and toward a path of destruction. It doesn't shy away from addressing the real temptations and struggles that believers face daily, offering a candid look at the consequences of fornication, both spiritually and physically. Grounded in Scripture, calls readers to heed the biblical plea found in 1 Corinthians 6:18, where the Apostle Paul urges, "Flee fornication. Every sin that a man doeth is without

1. https://books2read.com/u/3GLqln

2. https://books2read.com/u/3GLqln

the body; but he that committeth fornication sinneth against his own body." This verse serves as the cornerstone of the book, emphasizing the severe spiritual implications of sexual immorality. From the story of Joseph fleeing Potiphar's wife to David's tragic fall with Bathsheba, the book illustrates the importance of vigilance and the devastating consequences of yielding to temptation. It also highlights the power of God's grace and the importance of repentance and restoration for those who have stumbled. The book doesn't just focus on the negative aspects but also provides uplifting encouragement on how to live a life of purity, including practical steps such as setting boundaries, avoiding compromising situations, and seeking accountability. The author stresses that purity is not just about saying "no" to sin but about saying "yes" to a deeper relationship with God. By committing to purity, believers can experience a closer walk with God, free from the guilt and shame that sexual sin brings. The book also considers the role of the Holy Spirit in empowering believers to overcome temptation and live a life that honors God. It is a call to action for those who desire to live a life that reflects the holiness of God, reminding readers that their bodies are temples of the Holy Spirit, and they are called to honor God with their bodies (1 Corinthians 6:19-20). "Flee Fornication - The Plea For Purity" is a powerful and timely message for a generation bombarded with sexual temptation, offering hope, healing, and a path to victory through Christ.